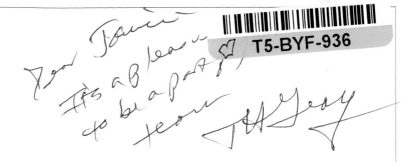

PRAISE FOR

Business Techniques for Growth

"How can a small business change to keep up and grow? This book explains all the levers, from employee performance to revenue growth and operations improvement."

—Mark Petrilli, State Director,
Illinois Small Business Development Centers

"Learn to grow your business and sell it, all in one well-organized guide for the small business owner."

—Jim Jaggers, President, Envirolutions Inc.

PRAISE FOR

Business Techniques in Troubled Times

"I found a book that really gets it . . . This is one of the best business books I've read that dives into the nuts and bolts of starting a growing a successful business . . . I read a lot of "MBA in a Box" type books, and so far, I've never seen a better integrated "All-in-One" guide . . . It's an action guide and a business toolkit . . . This book really packs a lot into it . . . There's a hard-core focus on getting results throughout the book . . . What's especially interesting is that the author is a turnaround artist. He helps flailing and failing businesses get back on track. Imagine having that kind of ability—to help businesses rise from the ashes phoenix-style. That's cool stuff. Actually, that's very powerful stuff."

—J. D. Meier, Sources of Insight.com

"This detailed book provides tools, techniques, and strategies for every aspect of a small business. There is real content in this book. It isn't a philosophical diatribe about the theory of small business success. It provides tactical, specific ideas for fixing and improving processes and policies. There's even a section about family businesses! I highly recommend this book, regardless of the economic times! One of the things I found most valuable is the way the book is structured. A small business owner can jump to a section where they are experiencing issues that need resolution, or they can read straight through."

—Diane Helbig, Seize This Day Blog

"I consider this book to be the "Swiss Army Knife" of success tools. If you invest in one management book this year, this book would be the one . . . the perfect foundational read for the new manager or entrepreneur, and a great refresher for the experienced. It goes from A to Z on what you need to succeed in a simple-to-follow way, including especially challenging subjects like working with relatives, salesperson compensation, and considering bankruptcy."

—Ed Sykes, The Sykes Group's OnPoint

"This book provides tools and techniques for people interested in starting a new company, and for successful companies now in decline. Choose to use the whole collection of tools, or grab the one you need.

Growing and exiting a business are often overlooked in business management books, but not in this one. Gray emphasizes focusing on the core product or service in growing the company. Expansion of core markets and products is okay, but keep them under control.

Maintain a financial analysis, and those sections not meeting return on investment targets should be eliminated. Don't let the competition drive your pricing. Differentiate your business from the competition by other means such as a better product or a better service. Make sure the marketing message conveys the difference."

—Bruce G. Smith, Seattle Post-Intelligencer,
Sunday, June 9, 2013

"I highly recommend this results-oriented and indispensable book

* Straightforward and useful advice . . . trustworthy and real-world-tested.

* Comprehensive and very hands-on.

* Clear and concise format, module-based, with an emphasis on simple methods that can be implemented with ease to get the desired results.

* Superb guide to resolving both short and long term obstacles in a minimum amount of time."

—Wayne Hurlbert,
Blog Business Success host on BlogTalkRadio

"The tools and techniques in this book . . . are perfectly designed to help those business owners who are focused on production to look at other aspects of their operations. What immediately struck me about this book that is different from any others is . . . one of the neatest and practical book indexes I've seen for a very long time."

—Mike Morrison, RAPIDBI

"Whether you're starting a new business, or experienced but looking for a deeper understanding of the concepts and terms your accountant and banker keep bringing up, you'll find the advice you're looking for in *Business Techniques in Troubled Times*.

One of the things that most impressed me about *Business Techniques in Troubled Times* is the way a complex topic has been logically organized for efficient reading. There are 2 versions of the table of contents:

- **Overview table of contents.** This provides an at-a-glance view of the book's sections and chapter titles.
- **Detailed table of contents.** This provides a detailed list of the topics covered in each chapter with specific page references within each chapter.

Business Techniques in Troubled Times also contains a visual table of contents in the back of the book to help you go directly to specific terms or topics. As a result, you can read the book from cover to cover to familiarize yourself with the basic topics, or you can go directly to the terms or topics you're dealing with."

—Roger C. Parker, PublishedandProfitable

"America needs this book! We need small business to succeed, and this book puts the right tools at the fingertips of small business problem-solvers."

—Mark Petrilli, State Director,
Illinois Small Business Development Center

"This book cuts through the fog like a breath of fresh air in a cigar-smoker's car. Clear thinking and clear explanations set this book apart. Tom Gray knows what works."

—Walt Catlow, Angel investor, Former Dean,
Concordia University Chicago School of Business

"70 techniques or one theory—which will help you more? Too many management books ballyhoo one idea as the grand solution for all businesses. But this book gives us 70 practical techniques, and presents them in step-by-step packages. When a new problem pops up, you just look up a different technique and follow the instructions."

—Brian O'Dea, CFO/COO,
Nephrology Associates of Northern Illinois

Business Techniques
for
Growth

MORE TOOLS FOR SMALL BUSINESS SUCCESS

THOMAS H. GRAY

Business Techniques for Growth: More Tools for Small Business Success
Copyright © 2014 by Thomas H. Gray Incorporated. All Rights Reserved.

For information about this title, contact the publisher:
Thomas H. Gray Incorporated
5131 Hawthorne Lane
Lisle, Illinois 60532, USA
tgray@tom-gray.com

Library of Congress Control Number: 2014902541

ISBN: 978-0-9886758-2-7

Printed in the United States of America

Cover and Interior design: 1106 Design, Phoenix, AZ. *www.1106design.com*

Foreword

SMALL BUSINESS OPERATES ON THE EDGE. There's no cushion. Owners know they need to grow, but resources are tight. Every small business owner asks, "How can I make the right decisions to build size and profits?"

Today's environment is changing fast. Business owners must deal with new technology, new regulations, and a new workforce schooled in the digital age. How will they change to keep up and grow?

Tom Gray's new book *Business Techniques for Growth: More Tools for Small Business Success* is a valuable hands-on guide. It uses everyday language to show you how to analyze your business, so you can see the opportunities. He examines all the levers to grow profits, from revenue to employee performance to operations improvement. And he offers practical tips for negotiating and decision-making.

The book explains dozens of simple and proven techniques in a clear step-by-step presentation. It's a "toolbox" of proven techniques. Plus, the book's modular organization lets you navigate quickly to your issue, like dipping into the toolbox for just the right screwdriver.

This book builds on Gray's first book, *Business Techniques in Troubled Times: A Toolbox for Small Business Success,* designed for start-ups. *Business Techniques for Growth* speaks to operating small businesses, targeting their need to build a sustainable and growing bottom line. Together, the two books form an invaluable set of clearly-explained real-world-tested solutions for the growth of small business in America.

How do you know you can trust these techniques? Tom Gray knows what he's talking about! After 30 years of improving results in the corporate world, he's been advising small businesses since 2000. Tom is an advisor certified by the Illinois Entrepreneurship and Small Business Growth Association, SCORE and the Turnaround Management Association. He teaches business to graduate students at four universities. He started his own consulting firm in 2001 and continues to manage it today.

As a business professional, Gray has been gathering and refining these techniques for many years. This book finally makes them available to a wider audience, and our communities will be better for it!

The Illinois Small Business Development Centers located throughout the state provide timely information, confidential business guidance, valued training and access to resources for early stage and existing small businesses. This book will be one of the resources we recommend.

Mark A. Petrilli
State Director
Illinois Small Business Development Center

Table of Contents

Detailed Table of Contents

Motivating people in America is about opportunity for achievement, trust, and then showing appreciation. It starts with getting to know your people.

Signs of disrespect drain the motivation out of a competent team. Techniques to sustain motivation begin with respecting the worth of the people at work.

Fair pay is important, but annual bonuses are better than base salary increases for the company and for motivation. Find the market rate to set salary levels.

Bonus motivates performance better than a salary increase, but can be harmful if it does not reward teamwork and company results as well as individual work.

Summary of articles on revenue growth techniques, from fast-acting quick wins to longer and more serious efforts. Which levers will work for you?

Growing profits with cost control is a safer bet than trying to grow with new customers. To get the full benefit from new revenue, optimize operations first.

To improve processes, look for the Eight Wastes. Here is a list of operations, purchasing, and management signals suggesting where to look.

The process map is the technique to improve operations. Appoint a team, choose a process, do a SIPOC, then observe and record on a process map. Great for teams!

Here are questions to trigger ideas for improving processes— a creative and exciting effort that builds team spirit. Estimate value and plan for implementation too.

Lays out simple and low-cost techniques to improve processes, based on these Lean principles: standardize, simplify, balance steps, pull, visuals, bottlenecks, continuous improvement.

Chapter 13: From Due Diligence to Closing

Due diligence is where buyers use documents to scrutinize the seller's assertions. Reactions to material findings can result in a price cut or more risk-sharing by sellers.

Use this ideal list of due diligence documents from the buyer's perspective as a basis for selecting the documents you wish to assemble for your data room.

Deal terms change after buyers find material issues during due diligence, if they do not walk away. Buyers seek to shift risk to the seller in several ways.

Closing conditions deal with business changes since signing, and post-closing activities. Buyers seek tight terms, giving them rights to terminate.

Disclaimer

This book is designed to provide information and techniques for growing and selling a business. It is sold with the understanding that the author is not engaged in rendering legal, accounting, or other professional services herein. The author shall have neither liability nor responsibility to any person or entity with respect to any loss or damage caused, or alleged to have been caused, directly or indirectly, by the information contained in this book.

Acknowledgments

THIS BOOK IS THE PRODUCT of my practice and reflection on successful business techniques for forty years. Along the way I was lucky enough to work with some excellent and patient colleagues, advisors, clients, and students in many companies and organizations.

These include Ameritech, Belgacom, FLAG, SCORE, Turnaround Management Association, Telecom Expert Group (my first consulting company), Mooney Airplane Company, Aurora University, Benedictine University, and Concordia University Chicago.

In the corporate world I had the opportunity to see effective and ineffective techniques and behaviors in practice, and I had the chance to make mistakes, reflect, and learn to do better the next time. Then, working with smaller companies as a consultant and CEO, I learned to modify big-company techniques and develop new ones to fit the needs of my smaller clients. As an MBA professor, my practical experience was supplemented by wider readings and case analysis, including real-world cases being faced by my students.

Problems led to solutions. Reflecting on *how* we—colleagues and clients—solved problems eventually resulted in this toolbox of techniques. This *reflection* was the key. Usually one just solves a problem and moves on to the next task. But if you take the time to stop and think about the way you did it, and write it down so you can use it again, then you have a *technique.*

The articles in this book all depend on this broad spectrum of people and experiences. But some of them depend on more specific advice.

Part Five, Selling Your Business, benefited greatly from the advice of Bob Fader, Senior Consultant at MidCap Advisors, a nationwide boutique investment banking firm. Ken Volz, a former colleague in several organizations, also advised on Articles 10.1 and 10.2.

Other sources are cited in individual articles.

I would also like to thank Michele DeFilippo and Ronda Rawlins at 1106 Design for their advice on the world of self-publishing, formatting, layout, and marketing.

Finally, as friends and colleagues all recognize, my wife Nancy Gray has been a constant source of common sense, good judgment, and loving support through all these adventures.

Introduction

A s a small business owner, you know you need to grow. You need more revenue to offset overhead. You need efficient operations to make a profit on every unit. No has to tell you there is little margin for error. You see it every day.

You know it's risky to remain unchanged. Competitors pass you by. Customers move away. Technology enables alternatives to your methods. But change is risky too. Growth means you have to change. And you know you need to grow.

How do you decide? Which path to growth makes the most sense for your business? Which has the best balance of risk and return on investment? When you choose a path, how can you make the most of it?

This book provides tools to answer those questions and grow your business. Designed for "hands-on" owner-managers, it explains practical techniques for growing revenues and profits, putting effective tools in willing hands.

This book builds on my first book, *Business Techniques in Troubled Times: A Toolbox for Small Business Success,* designed for start-ups. *Business Techniques for Growth* continues the thread, targeting the need to build a sustainable and growing bottom line. Together, the two books form an invaluable set of clearly-explained real-world-tested solutions for the growth of small business in America.

The book considers several ways to grow your business:

* Managing People: Results improve with high-performing and well-motivated employees.

* Growing Revenue: From quick wins to new distributors, new markets, and new products.

* Improving Operations: The fastest and least risky way to grow profits.

* Negotiating and Deciding: Key skills to choose your course and make it happen.

* Selling Your Small Business: The ultimate test of growth.

Each of these "parts" of the book contains one or more chapters, composed of a series of short articles explaining business techniques. The articles are practical, focusing on how to use the technique to find the right customers, keep them satisfied, and improve profits.

Though it can certainly be read cover to cover, this book is designed to be a toolbox, where the reader can select a technique to deal with a current problem. To enable this selective usage, a list of article topics follows the Contents page, and an Index of Topics and Techniques follows the Conclusion.

Readers who find this book useful are welcome to keep up-to-date with new blog articles published weekly. You may subscribe to weekly emails of fresh articles at *www.tom-gray.com/blog-2/*.

Growth will always be the goal of small business. Use this book to keep your business afloat and growing with proven techniques explained in a practical way!

Growing through Employees

HAPPY EMPLOYEES PLEASE CUSTOMERS and keep them coming back. Unhappy employees drive away customers. This is especially true for small businesses due to their high interaction between employee and customer.

In this book about growing revenue and profits, we begin with employees because their performance is critical to revenue (i.e. customers) and costs, the two main elements of profits.

The other reason we start with employees concerns risk, an unavoidable part of every growth effort. Risk increases with more complexity and less control. Fortunately, owners know their employees and can influence their behaviors more easily than they can influence prospects, customers, distributors, and suppliers. The least risky and most predictable lever for growing profits is managing employees so they do their best.

Part One Driving Concepts

- Motivation has three drivers: opportunity for achievement, trust, and appreciation. Demotivation starts with disrespect.

- Compensation is about more than salary. Frequent non-cash rewards and recognition are more effective in boosting performance than annual salary and bonus. However, when it comes to annual payments, bonus based on performance is more effective than salary changes. Pay for performance, not for longevity!

- People work best when they know why their efforts are important. Owners should have a vision for the business, and share it with employees.

- Then they need to have individual conversations to understand how the people do their jobs, and how to remove obstacles to better performance—the Breakthrough Conversation.

- Delegating an area of the business is one way to improve employee performance. People work harder when they have a feeling of ownership. Then hold the team collectively accountable, and reward them as a team too.

- Small businesses are notorious for lack of paperwork, lack of definition, and lack of training. Use proven techniques to set up your employees for success, both new hires and old-timers. When they leave or fail, the first place to look is whether the boss set them up for success.

- Goal-setting is another proven technique. Make sure the employee's goals move the company toward achieving the vision, and make sure they have some "stretch" in them. Then reward achievement of challenging goals.

- Link goals, measurement, and compensation to vision and strategy in a consistent "management system," aligning everyone's efforts.

- Special techniques for special situations: new hires, leaders in the ranks, and departing employees.

Techniques Presented in Part One

Topic	Technique	Content	Articles
Motivation	3 Drivers	Opportunity for achievement, trust, appreciation.	1.1
	Demotivation	How you show disrespect.	1.2
Compensation	Salary Principles	Not a motivator; find the market rate.	2.1
	Salary Increases	Market rate; fairness; not a reward for longevity.	2.1
	Incentive Plans	Plan design: standard and points approaches.	2.2
	Non-Cash Rewards	Best motivator; list of 30.	2.3
Improving Employee Performance	Start with Vision	Vision, Buy-in, roles.	3.1
	Breakthrough Conversation	Get to know employees; how they do their jobs; what obstacles; remove and measure change.	3.2
	Delegate	Why it works; write methods first; train; how to introduce; incentives.	3.3
	Train	First write the method; train and demonstrate; job aid; graphic for guidance.	3.4
	Monitor and Coach	Monitoring form and how to use it.	3.5
	Collective Accountability	Why most incentive pay should be based on team, not individual, performance.	3.6
	Goal-setting	Why stretch goals; how to handle shortfalls.	3.7
	Appraisals	Work to upgrade your best people, not your worst.	3.8
	Management System	Aligning measurements and rewards with vision, strategy, and individual goals.	3.9

	Hiring People	Job description, Interview, Orientation, and 90-Day plan.	3.10
Improving Performance	Manage through Leaders	Identifying and developing them; managing through them.	3.11
	Learning from Staff Losses	Three most common reasons why people leave; it could be you! Survey attitudes regularly.	3.12

Chapter 1: Motivation

1.1 Motivating People—The Most Fundamental Management Technique

Smart people have created hundreds of management techniques, and every technique is designed to get results, because that is the goal of "management." Managers get results, and they do it through other people, by influencing people to take the right actions.

We spend many hours figuring out what the right actions might be, but those efforts depend on a fundamental assumption—that people will *want* to take those actions. If they don't want to, they won't do it, the actions won't happen, so the results will not happen either. To quote George Carlin, "Ya gotta wanna!"

So the fundamental management technique is motivating people. The first step in management is understanding how to do that. The corollary, addressed in the next article, is to understand how people lose that motivation.

Sure, you might say people work to earn a living. Carlin also quipped, "Most people work just hard enough not to get fired, and get paid just enough not to quit."[1] But that doesn't explain the behaviors we see every day: people taking pride in their work, making an extra effort to please customers, and thinking about solving work problems even when they're not working. Why does that happen?

What Motivates People?

Research and experience both tell us that, for American managers, the most satisfying workplace offers

* Opportunity for *achievement*—to do something that makes a difference.

* *Trust*—being trusted to do things well, and being able to trust that one's co-workers will deliver.

* *Appreciation*—recognition and rewards for their contributions and effort.

In this type of workplace, people work to achieve goals they believe in, to earn and keep the trust of their bosses and colleagues, and to earn appreciation for what they do. These are what motivate people. These are the reasons people *want* to take the right actions. How does a manager get them to "wanna"?

Most motivation techniques focus on recognition and rewards, the appreciation element mentioned above. But what about the other two? What about achievement and trust? Can you motivate repeated excellent behavior by saying "Thanks for that great work to accomplish a meaningless goal—I didn't think you had it in you?" Not likely in America!

Before focusing on recognition and rewards, managers must build a satisfying workplace by enabling achievement, and by building a climate of trust.

How Do You Do It?

You enable achievement by setting achievable goals and removing obstacles. You build a climate of trust by

* being trustworthy yourself.

* training/coaching (if necessary).

* trusting employees to deliver.

* recognizing their success.

* encouraging communication, so co-workers know the importance of their own role in team success.

Get to Know Your People

The starting point is getting to know what your employees can do, what they think they are supposed to do, and why they sometimes are unable to do it or even choose not to do it. Then you can reinforce their special abilities and discourage unproductive behaviors.

You do this by spending time with them where they work. Get out of your office and dialogue with them—not just talk, but mostly ask questions and listen. Find out what tasks they like to do, what's hard for them, what they're not sure of, what makes them feel good, and what bothers them about work. Listen to learn their skills, what contributions they need from colleagues, the behaviors they value, and the obstacles they face.

To motivate someone, you have to get to know him or her and the job you are asking them to do. Then you can do the manager's job in a way that fits with their values and context: explain what you need and why, assign tasks and build teams, train and coach, remove obstacles, foster communication. They will listen if you talk in their terms about their needs.

Then the results will come, and then you can show appreciation to reinforce the right behaviors. They will know they've done well, and they want to know that you see it too. As long as they know that, most of their motivation will come from inside. They'll *want* to continue to achieve and be worthy of trust.

No it's never done. There is always more you can do to make them "wanna." But it starts with knowing them, putting them in a position to succeed, trusting them to do so, and recognizing their efforts and success.

1.2 Demotivation Starts with Disrespect

Workplace motivation is based on achievement, trust, and then appreciation. Good managers build this kind of workplace, but we are only as good as our last interaction. Every manager slips now and then. This article considers the slips that matter most, and the recovery techniques that minimize the damage.

The boss controls rewards and quality of work life, so employees are very aware and curious about the boss. While you may be focused on appraising them, they are always appraising you. They are looking for trust and honesty, as well as job knowledge and relationship skills. The quickest way to prevent motivation, to suck it right out of a competent team, is to undervalue their contributions, the obstacles they must overcome, their abilities, and their intelligence.

Signs of Disrespect

How do they spot this lack of respect?

* They see arrogance when a boss refuses to listen and acknowledge what he (or she) doesn't know. It's better if he respects the hard-earned knowledge of his people, and admits he does not yet have that "tribal knowledge."

* They see dishonesty when a boss denies making an error or that he (or she) made that offensive comment. If she lies about that, what else does she lie about? It's better if the boss admits mistakes, since we all make them.

* They feel undervalued when a boss does not apologize for making errors that create rework. Expecting people to "own up" to their own behaviors is a two-way street. If the boss expects his (or her) people to be responsible and accountable, he or she must model that behavior.

* They also feel undervalued when they see a boss being "too busy" to be interested in his or her people: their challenges; their solutions; where they need help. Your calendar reveals what you value. Do you make time to talk to your people? If you claim to value their work, and then treat them like furniture, they see you as distant, arrogant, and most of all dishonest.

To de-motivate someone, all it takes is to promise but not deliver, or fail to behave the way you want them to behave.

Sustaining Motivation

Are there some basic behaviors that can help? Certainly! It's not a trendy useless list of the top ten! The basic behavior is this: *respect the worth of the people at work.*

Is that too simple? "Is that all there is?" Well, there's a lot in this idea. If you respect my worth, then:

* You assume I come to work each day planning to do a good job; you don't need to "police" me when I have a record of competence. Guidelines, standards, and references are sufficient.

* You praise me publicly when I do well; you protect my image and self-esteem by correcting and coaching me in private.

* You find opportunities to enable me to achieve.

* You find ways to show your trust in my abilities and judgment.

* You admit when you are wrong. You respect me enough to know I'm smart enough to know it already, but I want to see if you realize you're wrong.

* You say "I'm sorry" when you make a mistake or fall short of the ideal we both aspire to. It shows you respect me enough to value my esteem, so you apologize when you don't measure up.

* You ask for my help when you don't have all the information you need. You listen when I give it, and dialogue with me to see how it solves or does not solve the problem. You're willing to work with me—my contributions are worth that.

- When I ask you and you don't know, you say so, rather than making up an answer you may have to revise later. Then you find out and get back to me. I'm worth that follow-up effort.

A boss who respects the people at work trusts them to do their jobs well and be honest in their relationships at work. But there's another part—he or she trusts them enough to be honest in front of them. We all want the authority person to show humility: to admit when they are wrong or don't know, to ask for help, to say I'm sorry. But that behavior is too risky for the boss unless the employees can be trusted to receive it in a positive and respectful way. Respect begets respect.

So what's the first step in managing? Get to know your people, and help them get to know you.

- Respect them enough to learn their abilities so you can help them succeed when they are asked for the necessary level of performance.

- Respect them enough to learn the behaviors they value, so you can deliver those behaviors yourself.

- Let them know your way of working and the behaviors you value, so they know what you expect of them and what to expect of you.

- Then do what you said: model the right behavior—"walk the talk."

Once you trust each other, then you can work together to make growth happen.

PART ONE: GROWING THROUGH EMPLOYEES

Chapter 2: Compensation

2.1 Compensation: Salary and Structure

Many believe compensation is both a reward and a motivator: "you worked hard—so here is some money—keep it up and more will come."

While compensation is certainly a reward for *past* successful behavior, its power as a motivator for the right kind of *future* behavior is much less certain.

Motivation is about more than compensation. We already know from Article 1.1 that people are motivated to work harder by (1) the opportunity for achievement, (2) by being trusted and being able to trust co-workers, and (3) by appreciation for their efforts. Compensation can be one of the forms of appreciation, but it can also be a de-motivator if it seems unfair or unattainable or out of one's control.

We also know pay matters, not just for the dollars involved, but also for the signals it sends. These include appreciation and reinforcement of the right behaviors, such as teamwork, initiative, prudent and timely decisions, and achieving goals or targets.

This article offers a few principles for salary and compensation structure. Following articles will cover incentive plans and noncash incentives.

Guiding Principles for Salary at Hiring

1. Salary at hiring is not a motivator. It does not reward or reinforce future behavior.

2. Salary at hiring should be based on the market, i.e. what others pay for the same responsibilities and indicators of likely competence (experience, degree). Pay your employees between 80 and 120% of the average or median for the job title, depending on indicators of their competence.

3. How do you know what the market pays? Go to salary. com for averages by title per zip code, and to paypeeper. com for title, company and exact amount posted by individuals. Unfortunately, these sources do not distinguish between salary and bonus, and they do not reflect individual differences such as experience. Another source is college placement services. These may quote average and starting salaries, which can indicate the impact of experience on salary level.

4. If you want part of the compensation to be paid as a performance-based incentive payment, such as 20%, and you pay base salary at 100% of market, then total

compensation will be 120% of market. Some firms solve this by paying less than 100% of market for base salary, so that total compensation is 100–110% of the market rate. "Market" means the median salary for that title in your zip code.

Guiding Principles for Salary Increases

1. An increase in salary is *not* the best motivator for future performance. Increases tend to be accepted and banked or spent, and then forgotten when it comes time to decide how to behave at work. Once received, employees see them as an entitlement, because there is little likelihood that base salary will be reduced for poorer performance the next year.

2. As a result, businesses today realize their best course is to pay for performance with annual bonuses or incentives, not increases in base salary. This retains flexibility, rewards past success, and creates an incentive for future performance.

3. The right basis for a salary increase is the same as the basis for the salary at hiring: a change in what others would pay for this person's work. This would be a change in the market rate (perhaps due to inflation, i.e. higher cost of living), or a change in the person's ability to get results relative to their peers.

4. Duration of employment or "length of service" is not in itself a good reason for a salary increase. However, if those years on the payroll result in getting better results than a new hire, the better results are a reason to pay more than the hiring salary. Age does not earn

rewards; results do. This means the employer needs to have measurable objectives or standards of performance, understood by the employee, to decide whether an increase is merited.

5. The perception of fairness is all-important. The fairness test is "equal pay for equal value work." Without it, compensation can quickly become a *de*motivator. This is one reason for using *external* benchmarks for starting salary and raises. Fairness is also the reason for basing compensation on objective measures, such as % of targets achieved or the raw amount of production. The message should be that salary depends on the value of the employee to the business, as measured by how much others would pay for their skills. This is fairness.

Some would disagree. For example, if one person has four children and another has none, should the first person's higher living expenses be a reason to pay them more? But what if the second person was supporting a parent in a retirement home? Should physical weakness or mental instability be a reason to pay less? The exceptions are endless, and may even involve legal liability. Every decision motivated by compassion can appear unfair to other employees or courts. Remember: fairness is "equal pay for equal value work." This is why using objective standards for pay treatment is the best technique.

2.2 Small Business Incentive Plans

In the film *Caddyshack*, Carl (Bill Murray) reports that after he caddied for the Dalai Lama, he asked for a tip: "'Hey, Lama, hey, how about a little something, you know, for the effort, you know.' And the Lama says, 'Oh, uh, there won't be any money, but when you die, on your deathbed, you will receive total consciousness.' So I got that goin' for me, which is nice."[2] The Lama offered no cash. And then there's the boss who growls, "You get to keep your job."

Incentive plans are supposed to be win-win for company and for employee. But many plans fail to improve company results, and even create demotivation when they seem to be unfair or unattainable.

Appreciation is one of the three things that define a great workplace. In a small business, employees are the most important source of customer satisfaction. Happy employees make for happy customers. You can show appreciation with non-cash recognition and rewards. Many studies show these are more effective than cash bonus plans.

When you decide to use compensation to show appreciation, we have also noted in Article 2.1 that bonuses are the preferred way to increase compensation, rather than increases in base salary.

Designing a bonus or incentive plan takes some careful thought. This article describes how to do that. It excludes sales force compensation, which was covered in *Business Techniques in Troubled Times*, Article 9.4.[3]

Step One: Preparation

Decide the behaviors you want to promote, and the results you want the company to achieve. If you focus only on individual results, you may destroy teamwork and pay out rewards without improving company results. So every plan should reward all three levels: individual accomplishments, teamwork, and company results.

Each of these three performance arenas must be measured on quality or customer satisfaction as well as productivity. If not, your plan can cause quality to suffer when employees pursue productivity goals.

The plan must be simple enough to explain clearly, and it must be perceived as fair. Dimensions of fairness are:

* I do well when the company does well.

* I get credit for exceeding expectations (goals).

* I get credit for exceeding the performance of my peers.

* I get credit for helping my peers succeed.

The most effective plans deliver rewards frequently (e.g. quarterly, not annually), and their design enables the employees to track progress toward both goals and rewards.

Step Two: Design the Plan
Given the above principles, create the plan. Here is a classic design from a big company:

* Set a quality threshold that must be achieved to enable *any* payout (e.g. 95% customer satisfaction).

* For company results, you might pay a small percentage of company growth over the prior year's same quarter. For example, if the company grew 10%, the bonus pool might be 1%, or 10% of the gain. That percentage can be higher for higher level employees.

* For team results, use the same "percentage of gain" approach but base it on the team's productivity.

* For individual results, set a target payout to be earned by completely satisfactory (but not extraordinary) performance, and a threshold below which nothing is paid. Then award a percentage of the target payout matching the percentage by which individual goals were achieved or exceeded, up to a ceiling of 120%, or even 200%.

One problem with this design is the degree of goal-setting and measurement required, which may not be practical for a small business. A points system is much easier to explain and administer. For example, if you are operating a maid service and you want to reward houses cleaned with no complaints:

* Supervisors get 10 points and workers get 5 points per house cleaned with no complaints.

* Points can be redeemed for whatever list of rewards you want. Management can adjust the awards and the points needed to earn them without changing the way points are earned. For example, the award might be gift cards with a certain cash balance. Maybe 100 points earns a $10 gift card. Make sure the awards are large enough to be meaningful, but this can still be a small amount if the awards are frequent. Ceilings are not recommended; you do not want to limit performance that improves company results.

This Points Plan offers easy measurement, consideration of both quality and quantity, shared responsibility for the team, and frequent payouts. The most effective rewards for motivating behavior have only a short time lag between behavior and reward. They are effective because the link to recent behavior is clear. With such a plan, you have also shown appreciation for behaviors that enhance company results, and you've increased compensation, without increasing base salary.

Step Three: Plan for Administration

Administration involves budget, eligibility, goals/standards, assessment of performance, tracking and publishing progress, and making the award. Your goal is simple administration!

Your budget for the awards can be based on a percentage of salary. This way you will know what you can afford. You can limit eligibility by job title and by time on payroll. For example, eligibility can be begin after a probation period for new employees, and usually ends when the person leaves the company. However, if the departure is the company's idea and not for "cause" (theft, violation of ethical code, etc.), many companies pay previously-earned but not-yet-awarded bonus upon departure.

Performance goals must be measurable and in writing. This is the basis for awards. Note: simply creating such goals can be a major benefit to a loosely-administered small business.

Then you must devise a simple way to track performance and compare it to the goals. One example would be to spot-check each team's work using a standard checklist, in addition to counting the units of work completed.

The incentive plan is not an incentive unless people can see their progress and modify their behavior accordingly. This calls for a frequently-updated spreadsheet on the company's internal website and/or a poster in the break room.

The final piece to the puzzle is making the award itself. Quietly including it in a paycheck is a bad idea! You want to *show* appreciation, so make a show of it. In addition to congratulating and thanking those receiving awards, you want the other employees to emulate the best teams, ask them how they did it, and try to outdo them. That only happens if you create a periodic (monthly?) awards ceremony.

This public approach does not work well with the corporate plan described at the beginning of Step Two. Corporate bonuses tend to be confidential, because envy and jealousy get in the way when bosses allocate a finite pool of money. Also, the one rewarded can feel uncomfortable or even guilty, because her award means others get less. If the plan awards must be confidential, it is not the most effective plan.

In contrast, the Points Plan does not create internal disputes, because the awards pool is not finite. You estimated a budget, but you did not put a ceiling on it. Everyone can do well by helping the company do well.

2.3 Show Appreciation Effectively with Non-Cash Recognition and Rewards

Employees want to be appreciated, but owners want to do so *effectively*. This means the method is appreciated by employees, it motivates the right behaviors in the future, and it's affordable.

"Cash Often Falls Flat"

Many studies show that non-cash recognition and rewards are the most effective. This quote sums it up:

"As a reward, cash often falls flat. Employees given cash rewards quickly forget how they spend the cash, and most often the cash goes toward an unmemorable expense: bills. In industry surveys, 50% of cash reward recipients said they either used cash to pay bills or could not remember how it was used.

"In addition to being easily forgotten, relying on cash rewards to engage employees and drive performance quickly becomes a management challenge. Over time, cash rewards become viewed by employees as an entitlement, and managers run the risk of creating high employee expectations that cannot be satisfied. Soon, the denial of a merit raise, or a merely incremental raise, becomes a form of punishment instead of a performance-based reward.

"Another study found that when it comes to gifts, it's the thought that counts, not the price tag. 'The recognition that's conveyed through smaller gestures, perhaps done more frequently, is just as meaningful, if not more so, than large, splashy gifts,' the report stated. Simply accompanying recognition moments with a memento, such as a handwritten note, certificate, or desktop gift reminds the recipient about the recognition transaction and drives performance.

> *Recognition should be immediate.* For the greatest effect, praise should occur as soon after the event as possible. Delaying the recognition for a monthly or annual event diminishes the impact.

> *Recognition should be specific.* Recognize employees for more than a job well done. Praise them for the specific actions they took that contributed to the

overall success. Your praise will be more meaningful when it's specifically focused on the individual.

Recognition should be meaningful. Meaningful recognition ties the praise and gift back to an individual's personality, such as their persistence or attention to detail. It's important that the gift is relevant for the situation and the individual's personal preferences.

Recognition should be frequent. Recognizing employees every seven days is a key element to employee engagement, and it also opens the lines of communication about desired behaviors that fuel performance."

Source: http://www.baudville.com/Noncash_White_Paper/pdfs

The Right Behaviors
Whether the award is cash or non-cash, the boss first needs to decide which behaviors they want to encourage, and then be consistent in recognizing them.

Possible Non-Cash Rewards
Article 2.2 mentioned gift cards as incentives. Some other ideas include a health club membership, tax advice, concierge service, or even a weekend away. Here is a list of many more reward types to consider:[4]

1. Collate positive hand written statements about the employee from their colleagues, frame and present to the employee.

2. Provide the employee with some one-to-one coaching and mentoring sessions with a senior member of the organization for six months.

3. Register the employee for a conference or training session of their choice.

4. Share an inspirational success story with all and make it all about the employee.

5. Allocate a day in a week for them to do anything creative and of their choice for a month.

6. Give them a new job title or update their current job title.

7. Start an organizational "Wall of Fame" board in a prime spot and add their name to it.

8. Let the employee suggest a way they would like to be rewarded other than cash reward.

9. Pick up the tab to fuel their car for a week or a month.

10. Prepare, present, and disseminate a short video mosaic that celebrates the employee's accomplishments.

11. Get the employee some career counseling sessions.

12. Find out what the employee is passionate about and give them a gift related to it.

13. Pick up their family's tab for a dinner at their favorite restaurant.

14. Present the employee with a pair of tickets to a concert or a show so that they can invite their partner along.

15. Get them an iTune voucher if they own an iPod, iPad, iPhone etc.

16. Give them a day pass to a spa.

17. Present the employee with a handwritten thank you note.

18. Name a meeting room after the employee for a year.

19. Give the employee a reserved parking spot for six months.

20. Present the employee with a bouquet of flowers.

21. Make a public thank you announcement and give money to their favorite charity.

22. Arrange for the employee to take a fun class, such as jewelry making, scuba diving, or skydiving.

23. Present the employee with a tasteful framed certificate to show how valuable the employee's contribution to the company has been.

24. Give the employee a gift card to their favorite shop.

25. Get them a voucher to download eBooks from their favorite author.

26. Cover the cost to have a professional family portrait of the employee taken.

27. Allow the employee to be flexible with their working hours for one month.

28. Give the employee a day or two off work.

29. Get a mobile car valet service to do a full valet of their car.

30. Help to pay for a trade association membership of their choice.

PART ONE: GROWING THROUGH EMPLOYEES

Chapter 3: Improving Employee Performance

3.1 Getting Your People to Do the Best They Can:
Start with the Big Picture — 36

3.2 To Improve Performance, Have the
"Breakthrough Conversation" — 39

3.3 Delegate Responsibility to Improve Employee
Performance — 42

3.4 Setting Up Employees for Success, or Failure — 46

3.5 Is Monitoring Employee Performance a Lost Art? — 50

3.6 Collective Accountability: Preventing Delegation
from Destroying Teamwork — 55

3.7 To Get Great Results, Expect Top Performance — 59

3.8 Raising Team Performance — 61

3.9 Management System: Link Vision, Strategy,
Performance, and Compensation — 65

3.10 Make Every Hire Count—Manage Their First
90 Days — 69

3.11 Find and Develop the Leaders among Your
Employees — 71

3.12 Learn Why Employees Leave — 74

3.1 Getting Your People to Do the Best They Can: Start with the Big Picture

"Performance Management" is an unfortunate expression. The idea is good: getting your people to do the best job they can. But it's a big-company term. It's distant, condescending, and mechanistic—light years away from the mutual dependence of boss and employee that characterizes small business.

So let's focus on the idea, not the terminology. "Getting your people to do the best they can" is the heart of small business success. When it's working, everyone is satisfied—employees, customer, and company. Customers come back, and employees stay with you. Your business listens to ideas from both groups, so it grows by meeting the needs of its market. The business is healthy, and the employees feel secure and appreciated.

How do we get to such a beautiful place? This chapter shows the way! We'll cover accountability, goal-setting and expectations, tracking results, feedback, training, coaching, and more. But the first step is creating and explaining an inspiring vision.

Start with the Owner's Vision

People do their best when they are working toward an outcome that is not just satisfying, but inspirational: one that will make them feel proud. So the first step is creating and then sharing an inspirational vision for the company, a vision in tune with employees' values.

Their values are probably similar to yours. At the basic level, they value family, integrity, and trust. Going a step higher, they value professional competence, fair treatment of others, and financial success and security. At the highest level, they value the betterment of people and community, and the personal satisfaction of making a difference in achieving that improvement.

They value "doing things right," but they get inspired by "doing the right things."

So an inspirational vision pictures a company succeeding by improving the lives of people around them, and doing it in a smoothly competent way.

The owner is responsible for orchestrating the vision together with his or her key people. Why are we in this business? What are we trying to accomplish, and become? The vision is a multidimensional company description, set three years in the future. It uses one sentence or phrase to describe each dimension of that future company: customers, products, key processes, facilities, cash flow, organization, employee numbers and skills, and perhaps other key aspects of the company *at that future time.* For more on how to create a vision, see *Business Techniques in Troubled Times*, Chapter 1.[5]

Get "Buy-In" to the Vision

"Buy-in" is a current buzzword using the images of co-ownership and investment ("buy") to capture the ideas of belief and commitment to Vision. Employees who buy-in accept the envisioned outcome as a good thing for the organization, and for themselves as well. Further, they are willing to devote persistent effort to achieving it.

Those who developed the Vision—the owner and key employees—explain to everyone else why this is the kind of company that will meet evolving customer needs better than competitors, and why that will be good for both customers and employees. The explanation is a two-way conversation, listening to concerns as well as explaining.

If the vision is inspiring yet achievable, the best employees will buy-in. Some may opt out, and should be replaced. Others may withhold buy-in awaiting proof, such as actions showing the owner's personal commitment. This third group requires special attention, with more one-on-one explanations and listening.

Explain the Roles of the Owner and Each Employee to Achieve the Vision

"What are you, and we, going to do to become that kind of company?" The vision can only affect performance when people believe in it. Belief follows from a (1) a realistic plan, (2) evidence of commitment, (3) knowing what the vision means to me, in terms of what I must do differently, and (4) confidence that making such changes is both feasible and rewarding:

- What needs to be done?
- Who will do it?
- Where will they get the resources and training to do it?
- How will the effort of changing be rewarded?

The explanation must *personalize* the vision to get buy-in. The owner must personally commit to remove obstacles and provide resources, and show progress in doing so. Each employee must understand how their own job will change, and how they will fit into changes in process flows within the business. Change is never easy, so the explanation must also change incentives, so it becomes uncomfortable to resist the change, and rewarding to work differently. For more specifics on how to gain buy-in, see Article 1.4 in *Business Techniques in Trouble Times.*

When people commit to achieving an inspiring vision, they will do most of their own performance management—they will do the best they can. This is why working in a start-up can be so intense and so satisfying. But we all know that start-ups make all kinds of mistakes as well. So inspiration is just the beginning. The rest of the articles in this chapter will cover how to help employees do their best, and how to support their efforts.

3.2 To Improve Performance, Have the "Breakthrough Conversation"

When was the last time you really listened to your people about what gets in the way of doing the best they can do? Odds are you haven't in a long time, maybe because you think you know the "excuses" they will make. If so, you are at an impasse. You are not satisfied, and they're not either. When they're not satisfied, they don't do the best work they can.

Human nature works like this: when the issue is your own performance, you first blame the environment that blocks you—people, processes, customers, technology, etc. When the issue is someone else's performance, you first blame that person. Obviously, the truth is usually somewhere in between. Your people often feel this way too. It's never their fault. The obstacle is always something they do not control and hence cannot be responsible for fixing.

You can only make progress when you recognize this subconscious blaming pattern, and take steps to learn what really blocks people from doing their best. As the boss, you don't have the luxury of simply blaming obstacles. Your job is to remove the obstacles, to do the fixing! To improve performance—both yours and theirs—you must get past the blame impasse.

The Breakthrough Conversation

To get the best from your people, you need to understand their work challenges. Only then can you understand their obstacles, and remove them. How many bosses understand everything their people do? "She does that in the computer somehow" is not good enough!

The conversation can start with "Show me how you do that."

Next question: "What gets in your way? What makes doing that harder than it needs to be?" The answers may cover the whole business: not enough resources; I haven't been trained on an easier way; the people I send it to are slow to respond; I do it this way so I can go home earlier (an incentive); constant interruptions make me forget to do some steps; our products have some shortfalls that we in the office have to make up for; our process for (whatever) is slow, bureaucratic, and paper-driven.

Swamped by this deluge, Question 3 is where you try to come up for air by sorting through it all to find the fundamental issue(s): "So which of these problems seems to be the most important obstacle to doing this better and faster?"

Now, focusing on the most important issue, Question 4 asks, "*How* does that obstacle prevent better performance?" The answer is a start toward solutions, because it brings into play what the employee himself could do differently (better) even if nothing was changed.

Question 5 looks at the bigger picture: "Why do you suppose we do it that way? Why did we think that was good for us, at some time in the past?" Now you are on the same side, trying to understand the objectives so you can achieve them in a better way.

Question 6 asks the key question: "What would be a better way, so you could do your job better and faster?" If you can think through this together, find a solution, and make it happen, then you have the employee's buy-in (commitment) because it's their idea. Their buy-in means they *have* to deliver improved performance when the obstacle is gone.

You make this more tangible with Question 7: "How should I measure the change in your performance, so we know that removing the obstacle is worth doing? If the change is quality, will I see fewer complaints or less rework or more return customers? Roughly how much or how many? Can we agree that if the change is quantity, the time you take to do this operation will change by how much?"

Conclusion: "OK I will make this change happen, and we'll see how it changes our performance. If this change works, then we'll move on to some of the other obstacles you mentioned. Thanks for thinking this through with me. I may come back to you to check on whether the fix we figured out really makes your job better—would that be OK with you?"

Payoffs from the Breakthrough Conversation

1. The boss seems human, which enables you both to talk more and learn more. A relationship starts, or is strengthened.

2. The employee feels good: "He listened to me, which means he respects and appreciates me, so I'm going to perform better even without the change, just because I feel appreciated." Appreciation = motivation.

3. When you remove obstacles based on buy-in that it will improve performance, you have the basis for accountability. You've sent this message: "The way you do your job matters to company performance (that's why we are having this conversation), so it is worth measuring and evaluating."

4. Results may even improve because the employee was right!

So if you want to improve performance, listen to your people and take action to remove what they perceive as obstacles, in return for their buy-in to do better once the obstacle is gone.

3.3 Delegate Responsibility to Improve Employee Performance

Good bosses influence employees to behave as if the business was their own—to take responsibility, and to act responsibly. When employees feel ownership for a defined area or function, and appreciate being trusted to manage it as well as the owner himself, they manage themselves, and you get the best they can do.

Why Delegating Responsibility Generates Performance

Here is the logic:

- Achievement and trust are two of the three key motivators. See Article 1.1.

* To achieve, I must have an area where I own the results, to "show my stuff."

* Trust enables delegation of responsibility, a great benefit to all unless the small business owner really enjoys 80 hour work weeks! And it works both ways: absence of delegation shows absence of trust.

* BUT, delegation of responsibility is a lose-lose proposition unless you prepare the employee and the organization.

* Given the tools to succeed, employees who are trusted to achieve shared goals for their own defined area become the most motivated employees you have.

* High motivation leads to high results, given training.

Preparing for Delegation

First, define the area of responsibility, the measurements for success, and target levels of performance on those measurements. This may be the first time the owner has created such measurements and targets, which in itself makes the effort productive. You cannot improve unless you know (1) where you are and (2) how to measure change, from that point.

Second, *write down* how you want the job to be done. Again, writing procedures is probably a first for the owner. The process of writing should lead the owner and the employee to reflect on how to do it better. The resulting improvements are another payoff from the delegation effort. Note: preparing a process map before writing helps keep your writing organized, and provides a tool to redesign the process for better results. For more on Process Maps, see Chapter 7.

Third, decide how to train a *new* person to do the job the way you want. What tools will they need, such as job aids, ready references, and right way/wrong way photos? You design training for a new person to make sure you think it through without skipping steps or assuming a base of knowledge that may not really be present in every employee.

Fourth, produce the training, and fifth, conduct it for the assigned person. Take enough time to do it well. The last thing you want is a failure in the delegated area! Your training has three elements: telling, practice, and then demonstration of competence by the employee. Even if you and the employee think they have the competence, make them show you! This way you can refer back to their demonstrated success if they later slip up, to remind them they really do know how.

This graphic sums it up (more on this in the next article):

Knowledge Leads to Behavior

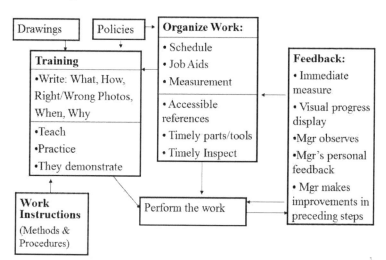

Last, prepare the organization. Anticipate process and relationship changes. Notify other employees of the employee's responsibility and authority, the reasons for the change, and the improved results you expect. Listen to their questions, and adapt as needed. For any employees where you expect major concerns, talk to them privately before having a group discussion.

Note: just as accountability without responsibility can be a cruel joke, responsibility without authority is more de-motivating than empowering. Delegate the authority with the responsibility if you want your employee to deliver his or her best efforts.

Follow-Up to Ensure Success

Once you have delegated the responsibility, be available for advice but avoid your tendency to do it for them! Don't micro-manage. Remember why you picked this person and this area of responsibility, and remember the competence they showed in training.

Your job after delegation is to share the results of the measurements, discuss ways to improve the results, observe, and coach. Be the orchestrator—don't play all the instruments yourself! One good way to avoid micromanaging and nagging is to schedule periodic observations rather than always looking over their shoulder. Then make sure your feedback is immediate and private, and deliver it in a positive but specific and useful way. Leave room for discussion of why the employee did what they did, and be prepared to change your measurements and training if their solution improves operations.

Team Issues

Expect some jealousy and resistance to the newly-delegated authority from some team members. Also expect some mistakes by the new "area boss," such as heavy-handed or timid actions. You will need to intervene to support the employee's authority, and you'll need to coach him or her on dealing with other employees.

When you intervene with other employees, the same feedback advice applies: immediate, private, positive, specific. Your message is that you all share an interest in the success of the business and its customers, so these must be the primary focus, not personal issues. High school and its judgmental cliques are over, and so is the time for indulging in destructive emotions like envy, jealousy, vengeance, and all the other immature behaviors people sometimes have a hard time growing out of.

Following articles will expand on three topics introduced above: training, observation and feedback, and team issues.

3.4 Setting Up Employees for Success, or Failure

Have you ever heard a boss moan, "How could you do this!?" When employees don't do what you want them to, your natural reaction is to blame the employee. Instead, a more productive response is to blame yourself. Ask yourself these questions:

- Did I make it clear what I wanted done, with what outcome?

- Did I make it clear how I wanted them to do it, or clearly state that the method was up to them?

- Did I make sure they understood what I wanted, and knew how to do it?

- Did I fail to remove obstacles to their success?

• Did I fail to replace bad incentives, i.e., rewards earned by doing what I *don't* want them to do?

Employees rarely set out to upset the boss! They often make mistakes with good intentions. This graphic provides a menu of actions to guide bosses to help employees succeed. Skip a step, and you are helping them to fail!

Knowledge Leads to Behavior

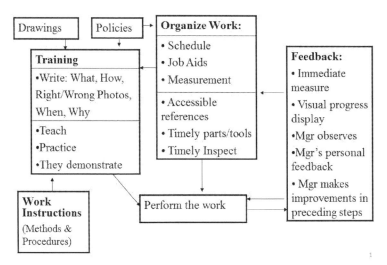

1. Define the Work

Discipline yourself to write down the way you want things done. This is unusual for small businesses, which may be a reason they stay small, and certainly contributes to chaos in the workplace! Writing is valuable because it forces you to organize your thinking, and because it provides a consistent reference. Before starting, it's best to do a little flowchart, called a process map, showing who does what when, with what inputs, producing what outputs. See Chapter 7.

Defining the work has three dimensions: policies, such as behavioral expectations (values); product drawings and specifications; and methods. You must write *how* to do the work. Employees should not be expected to read your mind!

2. Organize the Work: Framework for Success

Anticipate possible failures, and create safeguards.

- Schedule the work and the people so the resources (people, tools, materials) are available and deadlines are achievable without extraordinary efforts.

- Provide forms, checklists, and reminders where the work is being done. These are called "job aids," designed to help employees through potential trouble spots.

- Design measurements and progress indicators so employees know they are on schedule with acceptable quality. Make sure these indicators are easily visible as the work is being done.

- Create readily-available references such as right way/wrong way photos at the work station.

3. Write and Deliver Training

Again, small businesses rarely write things down. Training is usually word-of-mouth. As a result, training is inconsistent, and no training material is available for reference when employees are in doubt. They end up making their own "cheat sheets," which are usually incomplete. If you want consistency, write down your thoughts!

Training is not just how to do the work. It also covers who does what when, and most importantly it explains why you think your way is the best way to do it. Employees who understand the goal and the reasons for a particular method are much more likely to recall how to do it. Unlike automatons or lab rats, humans always want to know why! Take advantage of this trait to create memorable training.

Telling is only the beginning. They will remember only a small fraction of what they are told. Practice raises the recall rate dramatically, so training must include some supervised test cases where employees actually do what you told them to do, and the trainer coaches them through it. The third element to lock the training into their minds is the demonstration step, where they show you they know how to do it right without coaching. Now both you and they can have confidence they know how to do the job. Once you both have confidence, you can delegate responsibility.

4. Observation and Feedback

The best feedback is provided by the job itself. When you design the job, build in checkpoints and visual cues for interim feedback on quality and quantity. "Right way" photos are one example. Interim completion deadlines are another, such as "complete steps one and two in the first hour." Fail-safe indicators are also very effective, such as a parts kit where a missing part is obvious due to a gaping hole in the kit box. Testing the product is the ultimate visual cue, so provide the criteria for such a test, and make sure the employees can do the test themselves.

Manager observation and feedback will be covered in the next article.

3.5 Is Monitoring Employee Performance a Lost Art?

Remember the adage, "Hope for the best, but plan for the worst"? We know people want to do their best, and sometimes we can make the conditions right so they really will do their best. But how do they know what "their best" really is?

Have they been trained on the best practices? Even after training, how do *they* know they are really doing those best practices the right way? Are they experts themselves, after being trained? Not likely. Has anyone ever watched them work, and coached them on how to do it better?

Athletes know how easy it is to slip into a bad habit, whether it's footwork or the baseball swing or the golf swing. So athletes have coaches. Dancers have coaches. Singers have coaches. Do your employees have a coach?

Yes, this is the New Age when self-esteem is a goal in itself. We are very careful not to hurt anyone's feelings by suggesting they are not perfect. But the fact is people *are* imperfect—by definition, because they are human!

Previous articles explained that the most basic step in supervising employees is to ensure that employees know *how* to do their work. Those articles talked about

- Organizing the work so employees know what they are supposed to do.

- Documenting the proper work procedures and outcomes: drawings, policies, job aids, methods and procedures (detailed work instructions), process maps, productivity expectations.

- Training employees on this documentation and these methods.

- Making the training and the documentation readily-available at work stations.

- Observing employee performance and providing immediate feedback together with an improvement plan if needed.

This last step is often ignored in today's small (and large) businesses. For example, in manufacturing shops, supervisors keep busy fixing parts shortages. For a whole series of reasons, bosses rarely take the time to actually observe how workers do key elements of their jobs on a regular basis, and if necessary, help them get better at it.

Yet common sense and experience both tell us that humans are not perfect, and need to be reminded of how to do things right. So here is a classic process for doing that.

Use an Observation Worksheet

A worksheet for employee observations tells boss and employee what to look for in the observation. Here is one version. You may customize it for your own type of business. Copy and paste it several times to create a one page record of several observations so you can see patterns and progress.

Date	Product or Process	Task			
Accuracy	Speed	Skill	Tool Care	Product Care	Ovl
Corrective Action/Notes					
			Employee Initials:		

- Where and When: date and "product or process" provide employee and supervisor with the context. Time of day could also be entered.

- What is observed: each employee's job may include several skills ("task"). This form enables the supervisor to observe these skills one at a time.

- Assessment: the supervisor looks at accuracy, speed, and skill level for that task, as well as hygiene/pride issues such as tool care and care of the unit. (Care of the unit means that the employee does not scratch or otherwise damage or create a need for rework on the unit being processed.) The assessment can use points out of 5 or 10, or High/ Medium/Low vs. benchmark performance. A spot for an overall assessment is also provided.

- What to do about it: the supervisor enters corrective action needed and/or any explanatory notes after discussing it with the employee.

- Employee initials: the employee initials the form after the discussion with the supervisor, to be sure the results were communicated.

Set Standards

The company should set clear standards by task for accuracy, speed, skill, tool care, and unit care. Those standards should be expressed as measurements, to remove concerns about subjective bias in supervisor evaluations. In addition to describing ideal performance, the standards should define high, medium, and low level of performance for that skill or task. The standards should be part of the employee's training, so they know what you expect of them.

Regular Frequency

Schedule observations for a particular day and frequency in a week or month. This routine reduces employee concerns about special scrutiny, and makes sure you plan your time to actually perform the observations.

Employees with excellent skills and performance need not be observed as often as those who need help. For example new people might have observations once per day (different task/ skill each day); routine might be once per week; topnotch people once per month. Since each employee has many tasks/skills, the observation frequency for Task A may be different for Task B for the same employee, if his/her skill at doing A is better than B.

Feedback

Use observations to improve performance, not for discipline. This is the reason for the corrective action section in the form. Feedback should be private, prompt, and constructive. After corrective action (training) is completed, an observation should be done the next day, and again each week for a month, to ensure the improved technique is being used.

Supervisors must keep a record of their observations, as well as a record showing the corrective actions taken, when, and with employee acknowledgement. The supervisor's boss should periodically verify that the observations are being made and the corrective actions are being implemented, and that this is done SOON after the observation showed they were needed. Thus supervisors should keep a file for each employee with observations and records of corrective action.

Recognition and Rewards
Consider some event to celebrate excellence at a particular task or mastery of all tasks. Think of it as certification or a badge of proficiency. There could also be some bonus rewarding excellence. However, I believe a bonus is not necessary—the bonus is the reduced observations, since no one likes his boss looking over his shoulder! A financial bonus also creates an incentive for skewing the supervisor's ratings.

Fit with Delegating Responsibility
Earlier articles recommended delegating to motivate the best performance. This regular observation process can reveal when an employee is ready for delegation. It also provides the owner or boss with control to ensure that delegated responsibilities are being done well. The regular scheduled aspect of the process reduces employee concern that they are being singled out for excessive supervision. The certification element provides positive feedback and a sense of achievement, both important for motivation.

A New Age way to use this classic technique is to have the observations normally done by co-workers. Peer pressure can be a strong motivator! But even with this approach, the boss must occasionally observe as well, to provide quality control of the observations themselves.

Observation has its risks. If done in a negative or heavy-handed way, it can ruin motivation. But if observation is not done at all, delegation can ruin results, and the resulting lack of delegation can ruin the business as well as the owner's work-life balance. So the best business will marry delegation with a regular scheduled observation process.

3.6 Collective Accountability: Preventing Delegation from Destroying Teamwork

The coach says, "There is no I in team." meaning the team cannot succeed if the players focus on personal goals rather than team success. But when you delegate an area of responsibility (and authority) to one of your employees, you risk destroying the teamwork of people who see themselves as peers. Maybe the issue is jealousy, or maybe they take offense at the area boss's clumsy attempts to use their new authority.

Whatever the reason, the behavior from other employees can look like this:

- "It's not my job to make you look good."
- "I work for the owner; I don't work for you."
- "Who died and made you the boss?"
- "Do it yourself, Miss High-and-Mighty."

Meanwhile, the behavior of the newly-responsible area boss can look like this:

- "The owner said I'm in charge, so do what I tell you."
- "You always did a sloppy job, but I won't put up with it."
- "Do it my way or I'll report you."

The problem gets even worse if the area boss can earn a bonus for the team's performance, but the team does not share in the bonus.

Structural Conflict

In addition to the personal conflicts that arise in a small business, other conflicts are basic to any business. We'll call them "structural" because they arise from the way the business is structured.

Harold Resnick from worksystems.com puts it well:

> "Internal conflict exists in every organization. Cost and customer service pressures often push against each other. Sales and profitability pressures push against each other. Manufacturing throughput and quality controls push against each other. New product development and short term profitability push against each other. These conflicts are inherent in organizational life and help create the balance that optimizes business results. As long as each person is held responsible for a part of the solution, that individual will seek the best results for his individual area."[6]

The problem with each person optimizing their own area is that the team—the business—has no way to resolve conflicts other than escalating everything to the owner for a decision. Those who lose that argument may become dissatisfied, further weakening any teamwork that remained. Meanwhile business operations as a whole become much less efficient and customer-focused than if the owner did it all himself. Then he wonders why he delegated any responsibility in the first place!

Solution: Collective Accountability

The solution is to link consequences to collective results. A small part of rewards (bonus) can still be tied to achieving individual goals, but most of the rewards should be earned when the business as a whole succeeds. This means that an employee's compensation depends largely on factors he or she is not responsible for and cannot control. The employee can influence those results, but cannot control them.

People don't like depending on someone else's performance for a good part of their pay, but the business only succeeds if everyone works together—"there is no I in team." You have to do your part, and help others do their part as well.

Resnick illustrates the point with two stories:[7]

> "One example is a company in which a group of selected managers were brought together and assigned collective accountability for the operational performance of their business. Individually, they represented sales, service, operations, and finance. Traditionally, they had each been held responsible for their own areas.

"The collective accountability was twofold. First, these individuals were still individually responsible for their own functional areas. Secondly, they were now held collectively accountable for the monthly operational business results. It was their job to make the day-to-day balancing decisions to optimize the business using their collective functional authority. The results were astounding. Conflicts that were previously escalated up to senior management vanished. Customer satisfaction increased dramatically. Capacity and throughput increased. And so did profitability!

"The second example is in large project management, such as design-build projects. Large projects in this industry typically have an initial concept and design phase; an engineering phase; a construction phase; completion and handover to the customer; and follow-up service.

"In many companies a project manager works with each of the organizations providing its part of the project. When problems arise, each part points fingers at someone else. Each group accepts responsibility for its own area, but accountability for the entire project rests only with the project manager. Breakthroughs can occur in this model when an integrated team is pulled together that represents the entire project and this team is then held accountable (rewarded) for the completed project."

Collective accountability linked to collective rewards solves the potentially-divisive impact of delegating responsibility. Adding this key technique changes the relationship dynamics among the employees. Now the comments are:

* "Do this well so we can make a bonus."
* "Together we will look good; let's both do our parts."
* "Let me help you with that."

3.7 To Get Great Results, Expect Top Performance

Remember those three fundamentals of job satisfaction: opportunity to achieve, trust, and appreciation? That's from the employee's point of view. The boss wants not just a happy workforce—he or she also wants great results.

The boss can set the stage for great results by setting high expectations for employee performance, and by providing the opportunities for employees to meet those expectations.

Expectations
You want your employees to behave professionally, help each other, think like an owner, and be creative in their solutions. So tell them that! Explain what that means in your business. Give them examples, as models to remember.

Regardless of their history, make sure they believe that

1. You believe they have the ability to meet your high expectations, and
2. They will be rewarded when they do.

Treat them with respect, and they will respond to both your confidence and the rewards. As Liza Doolittle said in *My Fair Lady*, "The difference between a lady and a flower girl is not how she behaves, but how she is treated."[8]

Those who need some help should have the opportunity to get it. Give them positive, specific, and frequent feedback and coaching. Talk about their behaviors, not their personality! This enables you to continue to show respect for them as a person.

Give them training and job aids. Help them practice by pairing them with model performers, by reflecting with them on how others succeed, and by thinking with them as you problem-solve together. You can even reward the high-performer for the improvement of the person they were paired with.

Rewards

When people live up to your high expectations, you must live up to the promise of rewards. Deliver praise and recognition. Set up a bonus program, and honor it. Make sure it has several levels, so the best performers get great rewards, and others get rewards as well. For those who did not get the highest level rewards, offer coaching and tips for success, and give them opportunities to do more.

Goal-Setting

Once you establish and communicate your expectations and rewards, sit down with each employee to agree on their own goals. Discuss behavior and teamwork as well as individual results. Have the employee suggest a base level of performance, and a stretch target. Make it "challenging yet achievable." There should be rewards for performance beyond the base level, but no penalties for missing the stretch target. However, missing the base performance goal should have consequences. Otherwise your expectations lose credibility with all your people.

The Boss's Job

Your job has two parts:

1. Enable your people to reach their stretch goals by providing resources and feedback. Their success will strengthen your business!

2. Set stretch goals for yourself, and model your high expectations with your own behavior. Your success will help them succeed.

This is the positive approach to managing performance by managing expectations. The opposite works too. If you expect little, that's what you will get. If your message is blame, people will behave to avoid being singled out, rather than striving to achieve. If you set high objectives and then withhold resources or rewards, employees will laugh at your efforts and seek work elsewhere. Don't be that boss! Don't just be firm—be positive and helpful as well.

A high-performance work force is the mark of a high-performing business. Expect it and support it. In this type of context, goal-setting gets results.

3.8 Raising Team Performance

Every set of workers has members at different performance levels. And every member can move up to a higher performance level, even your stars. What are *you* doing to make that happen?

Too many small business owners spend most of their time on operational tasks, rather than on their people. Tasks don't talk back, they don't have personal problems or emotions, and you know when you completed them. People aren't like that! People are harder than your to-do list, and maybe that's why working on the performance of your people seems to be the last thing you get around to doing. Yet your people are more critical to small business success than any task.

Assume you've set the stage for their success:

- You've developed and communicated a vision, and they buy-in.

- You've delegated responsibility, and created reasonable (collective) accountability.

- Processes are optimized; training is complete; job aids are visible; and resources are available.

- You've created recognition and rewards aligned with top-notch performance.

- You've set high expectations, and model them yourself.

- Your employees have participated in setting goals, both base and stretch.

In a small business, the next step—privately assessing employees—goes on every day. But, what do you do with that assessment? Here's a set of techniques to move them up a notch.

1. Segment Employees by Performance

A: Your star(s)

B: Potential to be an A with additional experience or coaching

C: Steady and reliable

D: Marginal; requires supervision; work must be re-done too often

F: Substandard; negative influence on the team is an open secret, sometimes acknowledged

2. For Each Employee, Select a Key Area or Behavior to Improve—One that Would Move Them Up a Level

Small business owners know their people well. So you should know their performance weaknesses, with a bit of reflection. Which one of these weaknesses would have the most impact on results if it were improved? How feasible is that? What could *you* do? Are you doing it?

3. Start from the Top

Resist the tendency to spend all your time with the worst performers. The opportunity to turn them into stars is a long shot. Focus your efforts on your best people first, because their potential to improve is the easiest to realize.

Ask the A player what they need to be better. They already know. Make it happen for them.

Help your B player understand the difference between B vs. A performance. Give them the opportunity to learn and stretch. Maybe you can pair them on a project with an A player, or give them their own extra opportunity or project to make their mark. Provide plenty of support as they stretch into that new role. Then watch them blossom, and give credit.

C players need to know they are C level. In today's world of protecting self-esteem, they may believe they are already at B or A level performance. Make your expectations clear, and set up a coaching plan for that crucial behavior that can make all the difference. But, the coach should not be you! You need to be spending your time with the A and B players, where the potential to improve results is greatest.

D players may also be surprised to find their performance is marginal and their job may be at risk. These employees need a 90-day improvement plan designed for that key behavior you identified. Assign them a coach, again not you. A strong B player may be the best candidate—this can be their stretch project.

F players should be removed from the business quickly. There is little prospect of a good return from coaching efforts. You should not have waited so long! Your credibility will rise, and the team performance will improve right away.

Summary

Privately assess your people, select one key behavioral area to make the greatest impact on their performance, and then spend your personal time with the A and B players, and with moving the F player out of the business.

Enable the A player; challenge the B player to stretch; be clear with the C and D players; provide coaching to both, with a 90 day time limit for the D player's improvement.

Acknowledgement: This article is based on *"Raising the Performance Bar"* by Harold Resnick of worksystems.com.[9]

3.9 Management System: Link Vision, Strategy, Performance, and Compensation

A well-managed company has all the players paddling in the same direction, toward the same goal. It has a framework that makes all the parts support each other.

* The foundation is the Vision—what we are trying to become in three years.

* Gap Analysis shows what we must do to move from today's situation to the Vision.

* Prioritizing the strategic projects to bridge the gaps produces the Strategy to get there.

* Key Performance Indicators (KPIs) are the most important measurements showing progress toward the Vision.

* Assigning responsibility to key employees enables progress, secures their "engagement," and provides job satisfaction.

See *Business Techniques in Troubled Times*, Chapter 1, for a description of the techniques to get to this point. This is an action-oriented plan, but it is still only a plan. Success depends on execution, and execution depends on motivation, resources, and rewards.

Project Execution

Projects get done with the classic approach: "plan the work; work the plan." The boss's job is to demand planning and status reports, intervene as needed with advice and new resources, adjust targets when new information comes to light, motivate the team, measure progress, and provide rewards.

Once projects are assigned, the project owners must provide a step-by-step project plan to the boss in a week or two. One of the first steps will be to designate the project team members, and make sure they (and their boss) accept the responsibility.

Every two weeks the project owner should provide an updated project plan, showing the status of each activity. Encourage revisions to activities and due dates as more information becomes available.

The boss should be sure to assign one or two projects to himself. These will be initiatives that he or she is in the best position to accomplish, such as HR matters (hiring new skills, bonus plan), and key external efforts such as managing professional advisor expenses and developing new markets. The boss should prepare a plan, and provide biweekly updates. She must be just as accountable as the other project owners, and they should see her biweekly progress reports. Her project management should be a model for all the project owners.

Targets

The company needs two types of annual goals: progress on strategic projects, and profitability. The goals should have measurable targets. The measurements themselves are called Key Performance Indicators (KPIs).

Once the boss creates those goals, in consultation with employees, then he must prepare a budget. This is a realistic forecast of sales, revenue, expenses, and profits for the next 12 months. It will provide some expenses for strategic projects, and also account for any expected profit improvements from those projects in the coming year.

Then the employees prepare their own "one-page plans" for their performance for the year. These are the goals they agree on with the boss: both base goals and stretch goals should be mentioned. These plans should focus on planned accomplishments, not mere activities. Types of goals are operational (KPIs), teamwork, external impact (market, customers, community), and personal development. Each one page plan will have a section for each of these four types of goals, with bullet points for planned accomplishments and the target level of achievement in each of the four sections. The boss must do his own one-page plan.

The boss reviews employee one-page plans for approval, making sure they are reasonable and relevant to Key Performance Indicators. This is where the boss makes responsibility for measurements clear to each employee, including collective accountability (see Article 3.6). Some measurements will focus on strategic project progress, and others will be operational, such as sales or cost control.

Measurements

Publish measurements of the company's progress vs. strategic plan and budget each month. Ask employees for their plans to catch-up if they are falling short. Change target levels of performance or add new targets if new information dictates. Manage the targets in a helpful way: avoid blame; explore reasons; coach for improvement; continue to show respect for employees and flexibility in how they should address new or unforeseen challenges.

Recognition and Rewards

Recognition for success should be frequent and timely. Rewards (compensation) should be quarterly and annual. Rewards should be based on accomplishment of results committed to in the one-page plan, as modified during the year for unforeseen developments, not for mere effort or longevity.

At the end of the year, discuss company results compared to the plan and budget in an all-employee meeting. Comment on progress and reinforce the Vision. Use this as the starting point for next year's plan, budget, and one-page plans.

Management System

Now you have a Management System—a framework linking Vision, Strategy, Performance, and Compensation! Everyone in the company knows what they need to do, and what results they need to achieve. It's about accomplishments, not activities. We call this "alignment"—everyone paddling in the same direction, helping each other with complementary efforts and teamwork. Here's a summary of the sequence:

- Vision

- Gap Analysis

- Strategic Projects and Strategy

- Owners for strategic projects, processes, and perhaps vendors

- Project Plans and Biweekly Status

- Key Performance Indicators (KPIs)

- Annual Plan and Budget

- Individual One-Page Plans for accomplishments and measurements

- Monthly Measurements

* Quarterly and Annual Rewards based on one-page plan targets, modified during the year

3.10 Make Every Hire Count—Manage Their First 90 Days

Small businesses do not hire extra people! When they hire someone, they know exactly why they need that position. But finding the right people seems to be one of the most difficult tasks a small business faces. You need the right skills, but also the right fit: attitude, reliability, behaviors.

Before Interviewing

When you decide to hire, your first question is usually "where do I find someone?" Instead, it should be "exactly what do I need this person to do, how well do they need to do it, what skills/experience are crucial, and what other skills are nice to have?"

In other words, you need to write a job description, define their role in your processes, decide the level of performance that is acceptable, and define how to measure it. Thinking through these criteria will help you choose someone with the best chance of being the competent contributor you had in mind.

The Interview

There's plenty of advice on the Internet about interviewing, so I'll just add five questions to ask after you've covered skills and experience. The answers to these tell you about the person, not just their history. They will help you decide whether this person fits your company and team culture:

1. What is your single greatest accomplishment?
2. What is your single greatest failure—the one thing you would do over, if you could?
3. What is your single greatest strength?
4. What is the single thing about you that you would change, if you could?
5. What do you do to relax?

The First 90 Days Are Crucial

During the first 90 days, you need to decide if this hire was a mistake. Certainly you hope not, after all the time and effort that went into your search! You have two tasks: do everything you can to set up this hire for success, and don't kid yourself that everything will work out when you spot problems soon after hiring.

Setting Up Your New Employee for Success

- Provide a thorough orientation. In addition to general information about the company, pay, and benefits, make clear your Vision for the company, and the behaviors you expect (values). Explain the employee's role in the big picture: how their department fits in, and what they can do to make their department a success.

- Make sure they understand their whole job, not just the basic tasks they will start on. Be clear about the expected performance level, and how it is measured. Then explain the training period, and how long it should take before they reach the competence level that you are measuring. This is the payoff for thinking through the job description, the role in your processes, and the standards for performance ahead of time.

- Designate a Coach or Mentor, a go-to person for questions and concerns.

- Schedule feedback weekly for the first month, and perhaps less often in the next two months. Ask them what they wonder about. Tell them how they are doing. It's much easier to change their behavior at the beginning than later on.

Act on Problems

When the fit is not right, you will see warning signals in the first 30 days. However, it's hard to admit to yourself that you might have made a mistake. You dread the thought of redoing all that hiring work. You naturally hope things will get better over time. Often they don't.

When you see problems, have a very explicit conversation with the employee, and tell them what needs to change. Ask them if they think the fit is right, i.e., is this the company for them?

See if behaviors become acceptable in the next couple weeks. If not, make the hard decision then. The sooner you get the right person in the job, the better off the company will be. You and your company don't have the time to "save" someone who does not want to be saved.

3.11 Find and Develop the Leaders among Your Employees

In every work group, one or two people seem to be the core. They understand the whole process, not just their task. They seem to make good decisions. Their peers respect them and want to know their views. Whether they explain their thinking or simply "make it look easy" with quiet competence, they seem to influence those around them. That's leadership.

An employee can be a leader without a title. Leadership is not measured by the position you hold. It's measured by the effect you have, i.e. your influence on others. An employee with leadership skills can use them to advance the company's goals, or to frustrate them.

Identifying the "leader in the ranks" is the first step. Then you can use that insight to develop the leader's abilities and apply them more broadly.

I once ran a small company where I noticed three pairs of employees where one seemed to lead the other person in the pair. I realized that to improve results in their areas, I needed to manage the leader, and the other would follow. One of these leaders turned out to have abilities we were not using, so we gave her more responsibility. She appreciated the recognition, and became a very creative contributor. Two used their leadership in a negative way. Once they were terminated and replaced, the performance of their followers was much better.

Developing Leaders

Not everyone wants to "be developed." But those who choose not to take on more responsibility are still effective communicators to and from their work groups. Make sure these leaders understand your thinking and your values so they can help with work group buy-in. You'll also want to make sure they are comfortable coming to you with issues that bother their work group, so you can solve problems before they fester and reduce morale.

Other leaders are open to the challenge and satisfaction of greater responsibility. How can you help them grow?

People learn effective leadership by watching other leaders, by practicing, and by reflecting on what works, what doesn't, and why. Formal training can supplement this process, but experience is much more important. As management theorist Mintzberg said, "Leadership, like swimming, cannot be learned by reading about it."[10]

This means you develop leaders by spending time with them to develop their abilities, both before and after widening their scope.

* You explain to them why you led the way you did, and discuss other leaders' styles (models) as well. Learning from models is the best way to train for effective behaviors.

* You help them reflect on which leadership skills are crucial at various levels of the business: hands-on demonstration and follow-up as a foreman; hands-off coaching when you are managing foremen; collaboration across functions at more senior levels.

* You assign them work where they must exercise higher level skills, often as part of a team. You coach them as they work on the project, and reflect with them about effective behaviors during and after the project.

* Then you assign more developmental projects.

* Soon you can assign them wider areas of responsibility, where they can "learn by doing" in their own area. Again, the techniques to ensure their development are coaching and reflection. One CEO said: "Among the elements of

leadership, 80% is experience. Our first line of offense is just to put them (promising executives) in a job."[11] You'll be taking a risk, but risk is the only way to gain rewards. An oil company CEO said, "You have to be willing to challenge people and always advance them a little bit sooner than you think you should. We drill dry holes with people, just like we drill dry holes looking for oil and gas"[12]

The Payoff

Developing leaders helps solve the small business owner's problem of isolation and workload/burnout. People are always around, but you need someone to consult with, someone who understands the business, the customers, your staff, your processes. That person can be the leader you developed. They can be the "sounding board" to help you reflect, and they can take responsibility so the owner need not do it all.

The other payoff is that you keep the best employees by giving them opportunities to grow, and by showing respect, trust, and appreciation. These are the crucial elements of job satisfaction. Keeping your best employees means your business keeps performing at its best, and that's a tremendous payoff!

Developing the leaders among your employees requires your time and effort. The payoff is a smoother operation, more delegation, better alignment, and all the other hallmarks of a well-run business.

3.12 Learn Why Employees Leave

Each employee is crucial to a small business. When an employee decides to leave, the entire staff feels the loss. The owner will need to spend many hours finding a replacement, and everyone will have to deal with months of disruption until the replacement is found and becomes competent.

Sometimes the loss is a good thing, creating an opportunity for new blood and growth for current staff, but usually everyone wants to minimize turnover. To do that, you need to understand why people leave, and then manage the business so people want to stay.

Over the years, employee surveys are consistent in revealing the top three reasons why employees leave. Resnick describes them well at *Workforce Performance: Know Why Employees Leave*:[13]

> "The number one cause of resignations is the employee's immediate supervisor. Most employees don't leave their companies; they leave their bosses. And the reason usually has to do with employees feeling that they are not treated with basic respect. They do not believe their bosses listen to them or ask for their input. They do not think they are given the freedom to do their jobs. They feel 'micro-managed.' These are the primary reasons why people flee a work environment. When turnover remains consistently high in a department, you often have a problem supervisor.

> "The number two reason for resignation is lack of opportunity. If employees believe they are dead-ended, they will start to look for greener pastures. If no one ever asks them about their career goals, they believe that no one cares about their future. If they become good at a particular task and then are asked to do the same thing over and over again, they

become afraid they will lose their other skills. When this situation develops, you have an employee at risk.

"The third cause is lack of recognition. Everyone wants to be acknowledged. Everyone wants to be told when they've done a good job. Everyone wants to be appreciated. Employees even prefer negative feedback to no feedback at all. Yet most companies provide very little feedback and even less recognition. They assume that employees know they are doing a good job, and are appreciated. But the reverse is true. When employees receive no recognition, they assume they are being taken for granted."

These three reasons for departure are the inverse of the three job satisfiers noted in Article 1.1: trust, opportunity for achievement, and appreciation.

Making People Want to Stay

1. Listen to your people. Have the "Breakthrough Conversation." Then act on what you heard. Remove obstacles and improve processes.

2. Provide opportunities for growth. Develop leaders. Assign a variety of tasks. Delegate responsibility.

3. Look for good performance. "When you see it, say it." Show your appreciation personally, and celebrate competence to the entire group.

Don't Depend on the Exit Interview

The exit interview is an opportunity to learn why employees leave, but don't depend on it. People often pull their punches in an exit interview. They have already "checked out" mentally, so they decide not to spend the calories to make your business better. It's not their business any longer. They don't want to cause problems for former co-workers, and don't want to tell you that you yourself may be the reason they are leaving.

Instead, regularly ask your people what they think while they are still with you. This gives you a chance to "save" them and improve the business. Listen without becoming defensive. They may not tell you what they really think, but at the very least they will appreciate the respect you show by asking for their views.

Another technique is to ask them what they think anonymously. Big companies use a survey. You can do that too with Internet tools like Survey Monkey. The weakness of a survey is that you cannot ask follow-up questions or explore a particular area in detail.

You could also have an outsider ask them what they think. When I'm at a consulting client's business, I am continually amazed at the candor and frankness I see when I sit down with each employee. People seem to feel more comfortable telling their story to someone they do not work with every day. Sometimes it's because their boss has not asked and does not listen.

However you decide to learn what your people are thinking, the important thing is to do it, and then act on what you learned by making things better. Understanding their concerns is the key to keeping your people!

PART TWO

Growing Revenue

Growing Revenue

EVERY BUSINESS WANTS TO GROW REVENUE. Part Two provides the menu. Choose your favorite growth dish! But while choosing, consider risk as well as reward. Think about growing through a series of activities, starting with the lowest risk moves first. With the experience and profits gained, your next move will be less risky than if you had jumped to it immediately.

Part Two Driving Concepts

* Growing revenue is a popular goal, but it's only a stepping-stone. The real goal is growing profits, which puts more tools into play. You can grow profits with levers other than revenue, such as cost control, process improvement, investments, and improvements in employee performance.

* To assess the potential and actual effect of growth moves, you must understand your income statement (P&L) and how each move will affect it, plus understand how long the various moves take to produce measureable results. The higher risk moves usually take the longest time to deliver expected benefits.

* Everyone wants Quick Wins: actions with low risk and quick results.

* Some low risk moves produce results more quickly than others. They all require that you change something in the way you deal with your current customers.

* Moderate risk/reward moves include a new target market (segment) in your current geographical area, and a new distributor or collector of end users.

* Major moves offer the highest risk and reward. They include penetrating a new geographic market, and launching a new product.

Techniques Presented in Part Two

Topic	Technique	Content	Articles
Growth Goals and Levers	Profit Assessment	Compare returns to other uses of your funds; calculate target return.	4.1
	Business Growth Machine	Understand levers for growth, and timing to expect.	4.2, 4.3
Low Risk Growth Levers	Quick Wins	For results in 30 days, use price increase and cost controls.	5.1
	Grow revenue from current customers	Depends on customer database. Consider loyalty club, merchandising, product bundles, volume packaging, promotions, and events.	5.2
	Change approach to attract new customers	Differentiation, positioning, new segment, credibility, message, customer experience.	5.3
	Promotional Readiness	Make a list. Involve everyone. How the team works.	5.4
	Competitor's new product	Raise prices when they do.	5.5
Moderate Risk Growth Levers	New Target Segment	Choosing an attractive segment.	6.1
	Finding New Customer Collectors	One relationship to reach many customers. Deciding what benefits you want and how much you'll pay.	6.2
High Risk Growth Levers	New Geographic Market	Assessing similarity. Using Weighted Factor Rating method to choose new market.	6.3
	New Product	New product development process.	6.4
	Market Research	Research reduces risk. WISC offers low-cost research on customers, competitors, distributors, patents.	6.5

PART TWO: GROWING REVENUE

Chapter 4: Goals and the Business Growth Machine

4.1 Profit Assessment: Is My Business Worth Doing?

"Is my business worth doing?" Stop and reflect, look in the mirror, and answer that difficult question. Maybe your spouse is asking it too. "Why are you doing this (to yourself)?" Is following your dream a good idea financially? Will people pay you "enough" for working on what you are passionate about? How much is "enough?"

How much are you putting into your business, and what are you getting out of it in return? Could you get the same profit from another activity with less effort or risk?

Two Components: Compensation and Profit

Your business pays you wages or a salary for working IN the business. It also earns a profit for you. Think of this as your payback for working ON the business. The company profit is your "return" for the risk of investing your cash and effort to build the business.

Compensation

You should be paid as much for your time as someone else would pay you, net of taxes—not the best salary you ever had, but the pay you could get today if you seriously tried to find a good job but did not hit the jackpot. This is the market value of your time. For example,

- Assume your net pay is 2/3 your gross. If the salary is $60,000, the net is $40,000, or about $20/hour for 40 hours/week.

Don't get caught up in counting hours spent working at your own company vs. the hours spent if you worked for someone else. Just figure they are both full-time jobs. The extra hours you put into your own business are the trade-off for the benefits of being your own boss, working close to home, avoiding office politics, etc.

Profit or "Return"

"Return" is shorthand for "return on investment," the profit opportunity that compensates for the risk of making an investment. Financial investments can provide returns or profits of 3 to 10% without many hours of effort. Typical returns available to "little guy" investors:[14]

- 3–4% return on an A-rated corporate bond; hardly any risk.

- 9–11% return on the S&P 500 stocks since 1900 (lots less since 2000, but more since 2009); some risk, but if you diversify and do not buy/sell on dips, you have a good chance of earning this return.

- 6.5% return on a portfolio that is weighted 50/50 for the above two investment types.

You can get these returns by making a few phone calls and getting some good advice. You'll also need to spend a couple hours per month evaluating how you're doing. Yes, there is risk, but there is risk when you invest in a small business too. Which has greater risk: your local bakery, or the value investors place on a Fortune 500 company with lots of resources?

Now compare these profits from investing vs. the profits available from your small business. You invest your own cash and borrow money as well, making a personal guarantee to pay it back with interest. You can never be sure the business will produce enough cash to keep the doors open and the staff paid. For that kind of risk, what return makes it worthwhile?

If investing in a Fortune 500 company earns you 10% return with much less risk than running your own business, your small company should generate a higher return due to higher risk. 20% is a good target. This is 20% annually on the cash and debt you used to start and run the business, not 20% on revenue.

Example

Susan was laid off from a $90,000/year job. She thinks she could make $60,000 as an office manager somewhere, which is $40,000 net. Instead, she wants to open her own boutique in her town. The business plan calls for her to invest $50,000 cash, and take out a business loan (personally-guaranteed) of $150,000. What should she earn from her business to make it worth the effort?

When the business is mature (perhaps in year three), her salary should net her $40,000 based on her own market value as an employee, and the annual business profits (after interest but before repaying principal) should be another $40,000, based on $200,000 invested x 20% return for risk.

What If Your Business or Business Plan Falls Short?

The profit assessment is a trigger to action! It makes you review the ways you could increase profits. Here are two:

- Many new business owners are not sure what price level to choose. Target compensation and target return give them direction, so they don't price too low, a very common error we see in business plans.

- The other big unknown for a startup is the sales forecast. Your target profit can help you figure out how many sales you need. Then you can design a sales force and a marketing plan to get there.

4.2 The Business Growth Machine

Imagine yourself as the operator of a business growth machine, with dials to show changes in key business results, and lots of levers that enable you to cause those changes. You are the "great and powerful Oz"—the small business owner! Which levers should you pull first, and when will the results change?

Growth Techniques—Labels on Levers

Why does everyone want to grow their business? They want more profits (and less stress). They believe a bigger business will yield more profit.

Why would that be true? A bigger business means more revenue, yielding more gross (contribution) margin after variable costs. If overhead does not grow, that extra gross margin becomes profit.

If growing profit is the goal, then your search for growth opportunities goes beyond increasing revenue. You must also consider cost control and even additional investments to enable more profits.

This means you have three rows of levers: one row for revenue, another row for cost control, and a third row for investment. Each row contains several levers. For example, the *revenue row* levers are:

* Raise price

* Temporary promotion

* More repeat sales

* Higher purchase amount per sale

* New customers

* New distributor or collector/aggregator

* New market

* New product

Your *cost control set* has an upper row of levers for variable cost, and a lower row for fixed costs, also called overhead. The machine maker was nice enough to place variable cost levers in the row above fixed cost, so it would match your income statement! Your lever layout looks like this:

Cost Control	
Variable Cost	**Fixed Cost**
• Labor hours	• % nonproductive labor
• Labor wages	• Rent
• Labor benefits	• Marketing
• Material amount	• Office supplies/misc.
• Material cost	• Your salary/benefits
• Subcontractors	• Professional services*
• Shipping	• IT systems
• Sales commission	• Interest
	• More!

*Professional services includes consultants, lawyer, accountant, other outside services

In the third row—the *investment row*—all the levers have red handles. The machine-maker's lawyer even insisted on a warning label: "Use with caution! Misuse could destroy profits!" These levers include:

* Equipment—Buy a new machine (equipment financing).

* Leasehold improvements—Invest in improving the appearance of your location.

* Loan—Borrow more.

* Sell equity—Give a up a percentage of ownership in return for cash investment.

* Acquire—Buy another business.

* Divest—Sell a part of your business to get cash to invest in growth.

* Dispose—Junk and write-off facilities or equipment not generating profits.

* New Venture—Build a new business, such as a new product or new market.

Which Levers to Operate—What to Do Now?

Having unpacked this beautiful machine, you can't wait to start pulling levers. But first a wise advisor (maybe a spouse) suggests you check out the instructions. In the owner's manual you find this paragraph:

> *"Dear Great and Powerful Business Growth Machine Operator,*
>
> *Please be aware that some levers have immediate effects on results, while others have delayed impact. Also, the amount of growth caused by any lever depends on the external environment and the reactions of independent variables (e.g. people). If people do not do what you or the machine designer expect, the results will not be what you expect."*

This means you need to think about each lever. After you pull it, *when* can you expect results (machine dials) to show a change, and how much change, when it finally happens?

If you're in a hurry for growth (and who isn't?), you won't take time to read about each lever in the owner's manual. Instead, you'll jump right to the "lever impact timing" chart. Here's the chart for the revenue levers:

Quartile	Speed of Cash Impact	Lever or Technique
1st Lickety-split ("Quick Wins")	0 to 1 month	Raise price, cut cost, decide not to spend investment
2nd Pretty fast	1 to 3 months	Stimulate repeat purchases; motivate higher amount per buy
3rd Serious effort	3 to 12 months	New customers; new distribution channels
4th Long slog	1 to 3 years	New product; new market

4.3 Revenue Growth Techniques: Fast or Slow

As you decide which revenue lever to use to grow your business, you'll be thinking about what could go wrong as well as dreaming about success. You want some noticeable gains soon. You don't want a major effort for a minor or temporary gain. You don't want a major risk if smaller steps can deliver the same value. Let's consider first the idea of "noticeable gains soon."

"Quick Wins": You Have Control

Why do "lickety-split" (also called "Quick Win") levers raise your profits almost right away? For quick wins, implementation does not depend on others, and results are fairly predictable, especially if the moves are small.

If you look behind these quick win levers, inside your growth machine, you'll see simple and direct connections between the decision lever and the output gizmo. The owner decides, and it is done. Nothing is simpler than refusing to spend cash. You don't need an owner's manual for that! And raising a price has some risk, but it's easy to do.

You can sum it up with the word "control." The owner controls implementation, and the outcome is under control as well. Plus, if you have control, you can more easily "change the change" if you don't like the results.

In the Timing chart from Article 4.2, the owner's control of implementation and the predictability of results both decline in the lower categories. Maybe that's why they take longer to show results. But there are other reasons too.

"Pretty Fast": Complexity and skill requirements mean results are slower and less certain

When the owner cannot make it happen by declaring or giving orders, the lever involves some complexity. There are gizmos behind the lever to cause other gizmos to operate, so the outcome is more indirect. Anything indirect is harder to manage: harder to implement; harder to predict; harder to program. This means successful implementation takes more skill, and it also seems to take more time.

For example, consider the second row in the table: the "pretty fast" levers. To stimulate repeat purchases, the owner/machine creates a loyalty club and promotes it to customers in the customer database. This is more complex than raising price, because you or the machine must

- Create the loyalty club rules to fit the target customers.
- Make sure you have a customer database, so you know who to contact and how.
- Create a communications message and use media to pass the word.

- Then customers must pay attention to the message, find it compelling, and return to buy more

Even if you already have an adequate customer database as described in Articles 10.5 and 10.6 of *Business Techniques in Troubled Times,* three months can easily elapse before you see more revenue. The same kind of multi-step complexity affects your plans to get buyers to buy more in each purchase.

Complexity requires more time. The other variable is skill. The results you seek only happen if you have the skill to do each of these steps well. To the extent your skills fall short of the optimum, your results will fall short as well. Unlike quick wins, it's harder to predict the revenue effect of these "pretty fast" techniques or levers because they are harder to implement. As more complexity and skill are needed, control of results is less certain.

"Serious Effort": More variables and limited knowledge mean even more delay and uncertainty

The "serious effort" levers take longer, as much as 3 to 12 months, because you need to learn about new types of people and negotiate with them. You need to understand why prospects are not already customers. You have to learn which distributors are available, what kind of supplier they want to work with, and become that kind of company (see Chapter 9 in *Business Techniques in Troubled Times*). In both cases, you must then find new ways to get their attention, express your benefits, and make a deal.

The risk of failure rises when you move away from prices and costs you control and customers you know. You may do all that seems necessary and do it well (complexity and skills), but you may be doing the wrong things if you don't know what motivates new customers or new distributors. Hopefully the designer of your business growth machine (that would be you!) links the levers to the right gizmos, but if not, garbage in = garbage out.

"Long Slog": New products and new markets have the most unknowns

The riskiest and most uncertain lever, which also has a red handle, is a new product introduced to a new market. This is close to launching a new business, and the norm for a new business to reach cash breakeven is some time in the second year.

However, you can reduce risk and increase control by cutting the variables in half. A new product for *current* customers has lower risk because you already know their needs and how to reach them, and they already listen to you. This leaves only the product development risk.

A new market for an *existing* product has less risk because the product is known. Your challenge is only to understand how to reach and be heard by the new market. The unknowns/risks become even smaller if it is a new geographic area for the same type of customer you are already serving elsewhere.

Still, the learning and the many steps and skills involved with these techniques suggest that you won't see gains in profits for one to three years. It may feel like a "long slog." The projected profit gains may be large, but so is the uncertainty.

In sum, you will experience increases in time required, uncertainty of results, and risk of failure as you move along this chain:

Operations you control

    Current customers/current products

        New customers/old channels/current products

            New customers/new channels/current products

            Old customers/new products

            New customers/old products

            New customers/new products

Now ask yourself: "Which levers do I pull first?"

Chapter 5: Quick Wins and Current Customers

5.1 Grow Quick with "Quick Wins"

The ideal growth project delivers higher cash flow within 30 days. The increase is sustainable for months to come, it can be done within current resources, and you can stop it easily if it does not work out. If it's ideal, it also generates more customer loyalty and better employee morale. Does that sound like heaven on earth? It's a *quick win*. Where can you find one?

Hunting for Quick Wins

You don't have to look far. Take 15 minutes and think about:

- What would happen if I raised my price 5%? Would less than 5% of my customers leave?

- What items do I buy regularly that do not benefit my customers or my operations? Can we do without them? Examples: supplies, dues, donations, overuse of legal or accounting or consultant services, fees paid to payroll companies.

- What costs could I replace by using readily-available technology? Example: replace answering service with voice mail.

- Do I use suppliers where I've never tried to negotiate better terms? Have I recently analyzed replacing them? Examples: supplies, insurance, professional services, printing, computer maintenance.

- Can I order those materials or run that marketing program every two months rather than monthly with no negative impact on the business?

- What problems do we regularly work around? If I did it differently, would employees or customers appreciate the change?

Small Price Increase

If customers value your offering, a small price increase will not change their behavior, but can have a *tenfold* effect on cash flow: a 5% increase in price can boost profit by 50%, from 10% to 15%. See Article 8.4 in *Business Techniques in Troubled Times*.

Review the Expenses in the P&L

To see all your payments organized by supplier, use the detailed version of the Quickbooks P&L (Profit and Loss) report for the last quarter. Do you need that water service, or dues? Are you overusing professional advisors? Can you use your phone system or the Internet better? Is there an office machine that can eliminate an outside supplier? One client saved as much as 20% of payroll by canceling such spending.

Negotiating with traditional suppliers is another fruitful area. Call and ask for a discount, or ask whether they have a different package that might meet your needs better. Offer to commit to a standing order for a lower price. Meanwhile, contact a few alternatives to see if they have a better offer—new customers are the goal of every business, so as a new customer you may get their best offer. You can mention these alternatives when negotiating with your current supplier. One client got a 20% price reduction with a shorter contract length by "pushing back" on an initial offer.

Timing can be another quick win. Less frequent use of a monthly marketing program reduces cash outflow. You may also find ways to change the timing of payments so they fall into non-payroll weeks (rent), or are spread more evenly through the year (utilities).

Process improvements can take longer to implement than 30 days, but they can result in *major cash flow improvements.* See Chapter 7.

Wages can be another fruitful field. Can you reduce hours of operation? What percent of staff time is not spent on customer work? Can you use that extra time to provide a customer benefit such as product maintenance? If you did not have a particular support person, could you change operations so there was no major impact? Have you checked *www.salary.com* to see if you are paying more than the average for a particular job title in your area? One client was paying twice as much as the prevailing wage for one position, and also found a way to cut hours of operation by 20%.

Are there products or services where the margin (revenue minus variable costs) is less than half the price? If so, change the price, or reduce costs, or cancel the product/service, or bundle it into a higher priced package. See these articles in *Business Techniques in Troubled Times:* 7.1, 8.2, 8.3, 15.1, and 15.2.

Satisfaction Boosters

What problems do your staff or your customers work around every day? If you fix the problem, will employee morale and/or customer satisfaction improve? If so, the result should be better retention, better productivity, and happier customers who stay with you and even buy more.

Maybe it's a facility issue, like fixing a leaky roof, or painting, or moving furniture, or adding a postage machine. Maybe it's a process with too many steps. Maybe you require higher level approvals where you could trust your employees more. Maybe you could solicit staff input more often. Maybe you could use your office system to provide standard reports rather than interrupting employees to ask for status.

The Key to Quick Wins

Quick wins are the fastest way to business growth. Quick wins also boost morale and cash flow.

To find them, you just need to step back from the day-to-day grind and think about the business anew, as an outsider would.

If you were starting over, would you change the way you do things? If so, find a way to change now!

5.2 Grow Pretty Fast with Current Customers

Current customers are a "pretty fast" growth opportunity because you know how to reach them, and you can be fairly sure they will pay attention when you communicate. You know what products, features, and services they like. You know where they like to buy, and how much they normally spend. More knowns means less risk, and less time required for trial and error marketing. Your relationship with these customers offers more "control" than trying to reach new customers.

You want current customers to come back and buy again: repeat purchases. You want them to do that more often. And when they buy, you want them to spend more. How can you make that more likely to happen?

First, you need to capture what you know about these people, and make it easy to use the information. The tools are a *customer database*, and the reports it generates. For techniques to design the database and some useful reports, see Articles 10.5 and 10.6 in *Business Techniques in Troubled Times*. Now you can operate the growth levers.

Loyalty Club: More Purchases; Larger Buys

1. Tighten your relationship by recognizing their value— the Loyalty Club

    Name the club, define the threshold for membership, and create some offers to show the value of joining.

Then promote the new opportunity. When they join, make sure you note it in the customer database, and make sure your staff has an easy way to recognize loyalty club membership when they interact with these valuable folks.

2. Design some offers

   Hold an event just for them. Offer them extras, such as free maintenance or consultation using nonproductive staff time. Enable them to earn value by buying more, such as free shipping, volume discounts, one free product for every three bought, or special bundles of extra services.

3. Set up a regular stream of tailored communications to remind them of your appreciation.

Retail Merchandising

If you have your own retail location, arrange the store to show high margin products near the front and staples near the back, so customers see the high margin items as they move in both directions. Spend time to make the displays attractive. Train your salespeople to *ask* customers to buy the current special, or a complementary product or service. Make sure their offer is made as a service—not an irritation—to help customers meet their needs.

Bundles of Services

Package your laundry list of features and services into three tiers designed for common needs. Price them as good, better, best. Research shows most customers will choose more than the basic offer when three choices are present. The result is a larger buy, because you packaged the complementary services they may not have realized they needed until they saw the bundle. See Articles 7.1 and 8.6 in *Business Techniques in Troubled Times.*

The Special Combination

Apply your knowledge of how the customers use your product to create a combination of services they cannot find elsewhere in a single offer. This sets you apart from competitors, cements customer loyalty, and brings then back again and again. Feel free to acquire the extra feature(s) from other suppliers or contractors at a wholesale price—these suppliers will often offer you a discount for the extra business and your new relationship.

For example, the roofing contractor also does gutters and adds attic insulation. He employs the gutter crew, but he subcontracts the insulation to another company.

Lower Unit Price for Higher Volume Package

Your basic product represents only a fraction of your costs. The rest of your costs (overhead, marketing, shipping, job setup, some labor, customer service) don't change with the size of the package. This enables you to sell a larger package for a lower unit price while maintaining good margins. For example, your materials may cost only 25% of revenue, so you can offer a package twice as large as usual for a 50% higher price and still make a 50% profit on the extra revenue.

Temporary Promotion

All promotions are temporary. Create an offer that generates more revenue than the additional variable cost. The resulting sales margin boosts profits.

Hold an Event

An event gives you something special to promote and creates a captive audience for your sales effort. Those attending feel obliged to buy. The result is a temporary boost in cash, as well as an opportunity to identify more loyal customers.

Communication Is the Key Ingredient

Attractive offers without communications are a waste of time and effort. Like the famous tree falling in the forest when no one is nearby, they don't make a noise that anyone hears. Communications are the key to successful relationships. Your target customers must *hear* your communications if promotions are to succeed. This challenge is why building current customer sales cannot be a quick win. It is not totally under your control. But it can still be pretty fast, because these people already have a relationship with you, so they should be listening.

5.3 To Attract New Customers, Change Something!

Attracting new customers in your same target market is not just a communications challenge. A little "reinventing yourself" is needed! After all, you've been operating in their neighborhood for years, but they haven't chosen you! Why not? How are they meeting their needs without you? Did your message not reach them, or did they hear it but decide not to be interested?

You don't control these growth levers like you control your price and your costs. You don't have a relationship with these prospects, so you cannot build on it as if they were current customers. You cannot *make* these folks want to do business with you. Instead, you must first get them to notice you, and then get them to appreciate the benefits of your offer. This courtship takes time, perhaps three to twelve months. It's a serious effort!

First, Find Out Why

First you need to know why they haven't bought from you already. Do some research:

* Are they aware of your company? If not, how do you reach them?
  o What media do they use? How could your offer stand out in that media?
  o What finding words ("search arguments") would they enter into Google? Do your site's "keywords" match what they would enter?

* Are they aware but not interested? Why not? Do they not feel the need for your solution, or do they feel the need but believe another provider has a better offer?
  o Maybe they feel that buying from you is riskier than continuing to use their current provider.

Second, Change Something!

If they have not bought yet, whatever you are doing is not working for them. Don't expect different results from doing more of the same thing!

* Is your offer different enough to make them want to start solving their problem, or switch solution providers?
  o Consider your differentiation, your benefits statement (positioning), your product offer, your pricing, your accessibility, and your communications of all these.
  o Remember that your benefits statement or positioning addresses the value to the customer of your solution. Express it in customer value terms.

— For example, "a customer might say 'I want to protect my family if I die, but my financial circumstances change a lot and I need flexibility.' Few customers would say 'I need a universal life policy with a no lapse guarantee rider.'" Source: *Find and Enter New Markets.*

* One technique is to select a subset of prospects who share the same need/application of your product ("segment"), and target all the changes at them. For example, a special offer for seniors, or families with students, or people with older homes. You could address one new segment every six months. For more, see Article 6.1.

* Once you have a great offer, consider your credibility. Why should they take the risk of dealing with a new provider?
  ○ Build your credibility with a guarantee, testimonials, referrals, free or discounted samples, trials and introductory offers, and be visible helping people nearby.
  ○ Visibility tactics include press releases, participation in community associations and their events, and local sponsorships. These build networks and relationships. It's just natural to feel that "the company I know is less risky than one I don't know."

* Get them *to listen* with communications.
  ○ Find out what media they pay attention to, and when, and be there then.
  ○ Make your message stand out from the clutter. Deliver the message using a speaker they can identify with, solving a problem they share. Use color. Use the Web. Engage them with something interactive, like a free online evaluation, a contest, a video, or humor.

○ Invite a response. Your message must include a *call to action*. A limited time offer is a good trigger, but it must motivate them to take some kind of action: call, reply mail, email, website visit, free consultation, etc.

• The final step to get them to buy is their experience when they reach out to meet you, come to your shop, visit your website, or call for information.

○ Take special care to design this experience especially for the new customer with that particular need. Design the process and the tools, and train your people to use them well.

○ Build in a feedback loop. Ask them what made them decide to try out your company. Store that reason in your customer database, and tweak your offer and your communications to do more of what works!

Serious Efforts Take Serious Time

New relationships are a courtship. This is not speed-dating! You must choose the target, get to know them, modify your offer, and then find a way for them to get to know you. Expect to take three to twelve months to see the results.

5.4 Ready to Launch?

Success in launching a promotion or a new product is all about making lists. In a perfect world, you would foresee every way this new move could affect your customers and your operations, make a list of these issues, and have solutions ready to go. This avoids embarrassing and expensive discoveries after publicizing your initiative. Call it "operational readiness" or "promotional readiness."

For example:

- You thought to write down a return policy, but forgot to set up the process to handle the return.

- You find out customers are looking for a user manual, but you didn't think they would need one.

- Your publicity omits a key contact method: phone or email.

- Your order or billing system does not recognize the new product code.

Of course, the promotion or new product won't succeed if the target customers don't know about it. One client was considering giving a free fourth visit after a client had made and kept three appointments: four for the price of three. When asked about how long it would take to get ready to do so, he said, "Don't I just have to put up a sign in the reception area?"

Obviously he needed to inform the appointment makers and the billing people, but he also needed to send out the word to his customer list—everyone he wanted to make *new* appointments. The sign would inform only those already coming in, but his goal was to trigger appointments from inactive previous customers.

Involve Everyone: The Launch Team

Your employees know their jobs better than anyone else, and they know what customers ask for. To foresee everything, you need to involve everyone, or at least every department. If you are using departmental representatives, then they need to get the input of everyone in their department. Your company has the necessary knowledge, but it's up to you to draw it out.

The organizational technique is to form a team and make them responsible for successful launch. Make it an honor to be on the team—select members for their knowledge, communication ability, and organized thinking. Offer a bonus if all goes well.

Team members should represent all the functions of the business: marketing, sales, installation and repair, customer service, logistics, production, purchasing, engineering, IT, HR/training, facilities management, finance, logistics, legal, and perhaps others. Whether the business is large or small, the steps and the functional areas are the same, even if one person does many of the functions.

How the Team Works
The marketing person usually chairs the team.

Step One: In the kickoff meeting, it's the marketing person's job to explain the new initiative and its goals.

Step Two: Then all the team members make a list of what needs to be done to meet their department's needs. After discussions in this kickoff meeting, they go back to their desks and make a list of what needs to be done or provided for their group. Then they get the comments of their co-workers in that department, and take the revised list to the next team meeting where they explain it all.

Step Three: In the second team meeting, each team member explains each of the items on their list to the rest of the team.

Step Four: After that meeting, the chair assembles a master list, eliminating duplicate items and putting all the items into a sequence. For example, system changes must be completed before training can be done. This master list is given to the team members before the next meeting, so they have time to consider how to improve it.

Step Five: In its third meeting, the team comments on the master list and sequence. Then the tasks are assigned with estimated due dates.

Step Six: While tasks are being completed, the chair revises the timeline or project plan. The chair monitors progress and intervenes to solve roadblocks and assure cooperation. It may be wise to keep an issues list, where solutions can be written as well.

Step Seven: There may be progress-checking meetings, but the final meeting will be the one where every department "signs off" that all their work is done, and that everyone else has done the work the department needs.

Step Eight: Implement the pre-launch schedule. For example, confirm the launch date, notify employees and union, post new signage, etc.

Step Nine: Announce! This is the launch!

Successful companies not only have good ideas—they also pay careful attention to planning how to launch those ideas. Edison's famous phrase is "10% inspiration; 90% perspiration."[15] Sweating these details is critical to successful growth!

Nobody is perfect. There may still be some post-launch surprises. But pre-launch readiness minimizes the cost and embarrassment of post-launch adjustments. It is the difference between minor tweaks and scrambling to save the program.

5.5 Surprising Response to Competitor's New Product

When a competitor launches a new product, what do you do? Do you offer discounts, pump up your own marketing, or try to highlight competitor weaknesses?

The answer—what you *should* do—depends on what the competitor did with his entire product line, not just the new product.

Research shows that in many cases a new product launch is accompanied by a price *increase* for the competitor's other products in that product line. When your competitor raises his price, it's an opportunity for you to raise your price as well! So a new product can actually enable you to improve your profit margins!

Some examples were provided in "You Can Benefit from a Rival's New Product," by Raphael Thomadsen, Harvard Business Review, April 2013:[16]

- "In 67% of cases observed . . . Pampers revenue rose after stores added more kinds of Huggies diapers."

- When Yoplait introduced low-fat yogurt in the USA, Dannon sales volume fell 5%, but Dannon also raised its prices by more than 10% for a 5% net profit increase.

- When McDonald's franchisees open additional outlets, they often raise prices across the menu in all their stores. This is Burger King's opportunity to raise its prices and profits, due to a higher umbrella price level provided by its competitor.

- Where two major brands were in competition, Thomadsen saw the same Pampers/Huggies phenomenon in "40 to 60% of the instances in which one brand significantly increased its presence on a retailer's shelf."

Why do competitors raise prices when they launch something new? They want to create a price niche for the new product that fits with their other products. Unless the new product is priced above all the others, the prices for others must be changed to enable the new product to fit with reasonable gaps between product prices. These changes by the competitor are an opportunity for other companies to modify their own prices.

The cash profits from these higher prices can be used to compete with the competitor's new product, either by launching your own, or by intensifying marketing of the current line-up. If you raise prices as above, you can make these moves by spending new revenue. Otherwise, you will be dipping into profits to compete harder.

So when the competitor comes out with a new product, watch what happens to his prices for the entire product line, and then choose your response.

Chapter 6: Major Changes and Summary of Revenue Growth Techniques

6.1 Serious Growth: How to Choose a New Target Segment

Attracting new customers in your current geographic market need not be "more of the same." You can expand your customer base by appealing to a customer group who did not realize your product could be their solution. Such a group is also called a "market segment": a set of potential customers who all face a common need.

Article 5.3 suggested growing by targeting a series of new segments successively, one at a time. That article focused on how to modify your offer to appeal to new groups. This article homes in on how to identify promising segments for targeting.

Why bother with segments? Why not pursue the opportunity of the moment, one that just walked in the door, or that just occurred to the owner? Why not chase personal pet projects without comparing them to other possibilities in terms of their value to the business long-term?

You know the answer. It's about focus. Your resources—time, money, staff—are limited. If you spread them thinly across minor opportunities, your wins will be irrelevant to long-term success. If you spread them across several major opportunities, they will be inadequate to succeed. If you focus your resources, you can make a difference. This holds true for business, politics, war, education, and every other endeavor in our world.

Identifying a Potential Market Segment

A segment is a specific type of customer facing a particular circumstance. They have potential value to your business if you can describe that circumstance and how your solution is better. Use these questions to prompt your description:[17]

- What situation do they find challenging?

- Do they believe existing solutions over-serve, offering options that are too expensive or hard to use?

- What trade-offs do they make when assessing potential solutions, including the choice to do nothing? How well do these solutions rate on a variety of performance criteria?

- What is the value that excellent performance would create?

- What gets in the way of achieving excellent performance today? This may have little to do with a product or service in itself, but depend on the context in which it is used.

- Does the company have assets (brand, sales force, or intellectual property) that would give it unique advantages in serving these customers?

Choosing an Attractive Segment

A segment can be attractive if it is big enough to make a difference for your business, you can sustain the value of your solution despite likely competitor reactions, and you can find a way to be heard amid the clutter.

- Can you quantify the number of these types of customers? You need to know if the segment size is worth pursuing. For databases to help with this, see Article 2.8 in *Business Techniques in Troubled Times*.

- Do trends indicate this group is growing, not shrinking?

- Are competitors unlikely to respond with offers as good as yours from better-known brands?

- Can you imagine an affordable way to communicate with them about your solution and your company?

- Can you quickly find some "foothold" customers in the new segment, who can provide testimonials to attract others?

Technology-Based Approach

"Sometimes, a company needs to start from a different place—it has a unique technology and is seeking where to best deploy it or how to generate usage. In those situations, [the] questions would center on the unique attributes of the technology, who would find those attributes most useful, what constrains their consumption, what value the technology would create for customers, and what elements of the business model could be most powerful in unleashing growth. [Be especially conscious of finding] 'footholds'—small groups of customers that would readily adopt a technology, prove its utility, and serve as beacons to broader numbers of customers in the future."[18]

Serious Efforts Take Serious Time

New relationships are a courtship. This is not speed-dating! You must choose the target, get to know them, modify your offer, and then find a way for them to get to know you. Expect to take three to twelve months to see the results.

6.2 Growing through New Distributors and Collectors

Attracting a new distributor in the classic sense—a wholesaler, a reseller, one who sells to retail shops for you, was covered in Chapter 9 of *Business Techniques in Troubled Times*.

However, you can also interpret the word distributor more broadly. You are looking for situations where you can build *one* relationship to generate *multiple* customers. Imagine you are seeking "collectors" of potential customers. For example,

- A medical practice could attract an independent contractor who brings their own patient base and shares the overhead. That other doctor has already collected his or her patients.

- The same medical practice could become part of another insurance company's preferred provider list. That insurance plan has already collected its members.

- You could build a relationship with a community organization, a church, a fitness center, a team or league, an industry association, a school, etc.

All these groups have their own participants. When you are accepted by the organization, you can reach, or be presented to, their members or users.

Your website, blog, Facebook Business Page, and Twitter community are other distribution channels—each enables you to reach multiple prospects by building one capability.

The power of these relationships to generate multiple customers makes them worth an investment in time, personal effort, and financial consideration. You might attract these collectors with discounted prices for resale, commissions, donations, membership fees, and of course the cost/effort to make your website one of the best.

Forming Relationships with "Collectors"

Regarding social media, advice is everywhere. For example, Articles 10.3 and 10.4 in *Business Techniques in Troubled Times* offer these key points: organize the website by type of user; offer valuable information in your social media communications; "repurpose" your content into different social media; build your audience by participating in discussions and blogs.

Regarding other collectors, use a three-step process. Start with your own internal analysis, move out to research, and then reach out with personal contact.

First, decide what you want and how much you are willing to pay for it.

- You want:
  - Access to their members: list of email addresses; publication/website for advertising.
  - Opportunity for personal presence, such as participation in an event, speaking engagement, sponsorship, or posting your articles on their website or blog.
  - Status as a preferred provider, such as an endorsement.

- In addition to your time and expertise, you should expect to offer
  - Fee to join the association;
  - Sponsorship fees;
  - Event entry fees or booth fees;
  - Pay for each use of the member list for email;
  - Pay for ad in website or publication;
  - Possibly, a referral fee, sales commission, or donation.

Second, do a little research to identify a list of potential collectors, and then prioritize them:

- Are they local enough?

- Are they large enough in your local area?

- Do they seem to already have a relationship with a competitor?

Third, arrange a face-to-face chat, or at least a phone conversation. Face-to-face is best, because you are building a relationship that depends on your own attractiveness to them! In addition to verifying your research, you'll want to know:

- Are they willing to meet your needs? How strong would any recommendation be?

- What would they want from you?

Serious Efforts Take Serious Time

New relationships are a courtship. This is not speed-dating! You must choose the target, get to know them, modify your offer, and then find a way for them to get to know you. Expect to take up to twelve months to see the results. Building relationships with new distributors and collectors will take longer than attracting individual new customers, but the multiplier effect makes it worthwhile.

6.3 Major Growth Effort: Choosing and Entering a New Geographic Market

New markets and new products are major growth efforts. Which do you think is easier: entering a new market like the one you serve today, or developing and introducing a new product to your current market?

The answer probably depends on "how new?" How similar is the new market to your current customers? Is the new product a simple variation on the old products, and useful to your current customers? Both of these are easier than a very different market or a very different product. But both are harder than quick wins, more sales to current customers, and gaining new customers in your current market.

Selling current products to a new but similar market is easier than introducing a new product. As always, the reason is reduced complexity and greater control. New similar markets are easier than new product introductions because you already have a successful recipe for your market. Now you can grow by replicating it where conditions are similar. Replicating is easier than creating!

Before you start, think strategically for a moment. You should be looking for not just one new market. Your goal should be a *repeatable path to market penetration:* entering several new markets successively, one after the other, using learnings from one to do better in the next. For most small businesses, the vision will be *concentric circles* around the original market area.

How Similar Is That New Market?

The big mistakes and losses happen when you assume the new market is similar, but it has some key differences you did not plan for. Before even considering which new market to attack, take a few minutes to write down the characteristics of your current market. Some things to consider are:

1. Demographics: Age and income distribution, housing, education, literacy, etc.

2. Customer types: Anchor customers (e.g. universities), key industries, social groups

3. Regulatory requirements: Important if entering another state

   Note: this article will not address entering markets in other countries

4. Competition: Who competes with you? On what basis do they compete (price, quality, accessibility, etc.)? How intense is the competition?

5. Media outlets: Which ones are available? Which ones are most useful? What is their cost?

6. Local cost structure: Rent? Shipping? Labor? Are the skills you need available?

7. Supply chain cost: Shipping cost and timing?

8. Climate, seasonality, and customs: When do your customers buy, and for what seasonal purpose?

Choosing Which New Market

Assuming concentric circles, you can choose several nearby towns or metro areas as potential expansion targets. Now assess them for similarity. One technique is "Factor Rating." Set up a table with column one being some of the 8 factors above, and a column to the right for each potential new market area. Enter a rating of 1 to 5 in each box, with 5 being most similar to the home market. Then you can sum each column to find the most similar new town. The table might look like this:

Factor	Town 1	Town 2	Town 3	Town 4	Town 5
Demography	3	4	2	3	4
Cust. Types	4	3	5	4	3
Competition	5	1	2	5	2
Media	2	1	3	4	5
Local Costs	5	3	1	4	5
Seasonality	1	2	5	3	3
Total	20	14	18	23	22

After considering the totals in this first version, you may decide to weight each factor with a percentage, such as using 20% for seasonality and 80% for customer types. A second weighted version would result in a different set of totals, changing your conclusion about which new market is most similar to your home market.

Similarity is valuable to reduce the complexity of your entry, but here are a few other success considerations.

- The new market must be large enough to meet your goals, assuming a reasonable market share.

- Ideally, the new market should be facing some turmoil that makes people open-minded enough to consider new solutions from a new entrant.

- You should know the identity of a few key customers you expect to capture at the outset. This "foothold" will generate testimonials, referrals, and examples to provide the credibility that every new entrant needs.

- Supervision risk and cost: Do you know a manager you can use for the new market? Are there significant costs for transporting managers between the home office and the new market (airfare, lodging, car rental)?

You could do another factor rating table with these five rows: similarity, size, turmoil, foothold, supervision. For this table, weighting each factor is a must! Similarity gets the highest weight. Perhaps turmoil gets the lowest.

One word to the wise: do not fall in love with a particular new market because you found an ideal location there. A great location in a bad market will not grow your business. Pick the market first, and then explore locations.

Most likely, you will choose the new market for similarity, proximity, and profitability.

How to Penetrate the New Market

In addition to operational considerations, you'll need a localized marketing plan and a localized message.

The *marketing plan* will adapt your price, location, and communications to the local competitive and media situation. Referrals and anchor customers ("foothold") will be key objectives. Referral sources include the landlord, your vendors, distributors if you use them, and local "collectors" as described in the previous article. Of course, there must be a marketing budget and a sales forecast. Planning the launch will be critical.

The *message* for the new market will be a little different than in your home market, because it is pitched to the early adopters. These are the pioneers who will be the first to use your solutions. In addition to product information, your message must focus on earning credibility. Tools include introductory offers, videos showing people like those in your target market, and testimonials from the home market until you can gather some locally.

6.4 Major Growth Effort: New Product

Here's the vision: change and grow, or wither and die. The top companies earn 50% of their revenues from products introduced in the past five years.[19] New products not only enable growth—they also keep a business fresh and competitive.

But new products are a major effort. If you are doing more than merely adding a flavor or a feature to current products, new product development is probably the most complex growth activity you can find. Why? Because you are re-assessing everything that makes your company work, and changing many parts of it. You'll certainly change marketing, operations, and supply chain. You might also change organization, technology platform, and financing. Complexity takes time and adds risk.

To increase chances for success, the business must reduce complexity. The riskiest move is to introduce a new product into a new market, because the two new challenges (both product and market) seem to quadruple the complexity and risk of failure. Most small businesses are smart enough to want to do that only once—at startup!

So this article addresses new product development and introduction for your *current* geographic market. If the target is your current customers rather than a new segment of your home market, the risk is reduced even further.

New Product Development has three parts:

- Strategy: what do our customers want, that we could do differently than others, to deliver better value for customers?

- The process itself: fleshing out the details, while testing ideas for strategic fit, customer acceptance, feasibility, and profitability.

- Implementation and integration.

Before we start, consider two characteristics of the most successful new product processes.

1. The best process uses a team, representing all the key functions of the business. This avoids nasty surprises as you get closer to launch, and builds morale as well.

2. The best process plans ahead for the ability to launch *multiple* new products over time. This keeps your company in the forefront, and builds a growth engine. Envision a platform that can support several new products, and manage according to a *product roadmap,* so you know which products for which markets are coming next. See Article 7.3 in *Business Techniques in Troubled Times.*

Start with Strategy

First figure out where you are. Ask yourself and your team: what kind of company are we, who do we serve, what differentiation makes them want to buy from us, and what are the trends we and our competitors face?

Then ask, "What kind of company do we want to become?" Establish a vision for three years in the future. Define it in a multi-faceted way, so we know what to manage toward. The vision process is explained in Chapter 1 of *Business Techniques in Troubled Times.*

Describe the "platform" of technology and capabilities we will have then. What customers and product families can we use it to serve? How will we get the resources to do that?

Now that we know where we are going, we can consider products to get us there. This also means we will reject products that take us elsewhere. Call this "strategic fit."

The New Product Development Process

Trial and error has led to a well-developed set of models for new product development, designed to balance the cost and risk of failure with the opportunity for successful growth. All the models have *stages*, separated by *gates*. The gates are go/no go decision points, to decide if the idea deserves more resources for further development. These gates minimize wasting resources on ideas likely to fall short of the target criteria for success. Criteria might be market acceptance, size of market, production feasibility, and profit.

Eight stages describe the process. There are "go/no go" decisions, or gates, after stages 2, 4, 5, and 6.

1. Ideation: brainstorming ideas.

2. Idea screening, to identify the ideas with the best potential and strategic fit. What are your criteria to accept an idea for more development? You must be willing to use the same criteria to reject ideas. You cannot chase tangents with your limited resources! Now, decide whether to drop the idea or continue.

3. Concept development and market research is next. This stage estimates the marketing and operational requirements, and tests the idea with potential customers. You may prefer to skip the market research, but doing so adds risk. What if customers don't see the value like you do?

4. Now it's time for some numbers. The business case stage writes it all, estimating resources needed and profits expected. This becomes the standard for measuring success. Now, decide whether to drop the idea or continue.

5. Following a "go" decision on the business case, the next stage is detailed design, prototype, and market testing. Here is where you see if you can really do it, and whether people will buy it. Usually this process results in a list of changes you'll need to make! Now, decide whether to drop the idea or continue.

6. If the market test has good results, the company will spend the resources to make it happen. This involves most of the organization's functions, so the new product team must include a representative from each. Functional areas include production specifications, technical or software changes, manufacturing training and test runs, field operations procedures and training (e.g. retail, sales force, and installation/maintenance), and value chain readiness: suppliers and distributors. Now, decide if you are ready for launch.

7. Finally it's time for the Launch stage. Logistics, marketing, and training issues dominate here.

8. Tracking follows launch. What worked and what didn't? Are we meeting objectives from the business case? Why not? If you learn from your mistakes, you can improve not only the product, but the whole process as well. This reduces risk when launching the next new product.

New Product Implementation and Integration

The launch usually involves compromises and shortcuts to meet a target date, as the best-laid plans are frustrated by the real world. This last part of the effort may involve several months of feverish work to smoothly integrate new product production and marketing into the company's traditional processes.

The risks are high, but so is the opportunity. It won't happen fast. This step-by-step process has the best chance of managing the complexity, using resources most effectively on the best ideas.

6.5 The Three R's for Developing New Products

Flying blind into the marketplace can produce some nasty collisions. How can you learn enough about your product's market, so you can make smart decisions about whether to spend more money to launch that new product?

The 3R mantra is "**R**esearch **R**educes **R**isk." Market research is not reserved for big companies, and it needn't cost much if you use the Wisconsin Innovation Service Center at UW-Whitewater.[20] It's not limited to Wisconsin residents, and gets great reviews from entrepreneurs and inventors.

What can you get from WISC? First, you get confidentiality. Second, you get professional analysis of your product and its customers, distributors, licensors, and competitors to open your eyes to the real market you'll be entering. Third, you get credibility: these outside analyses make you and your product more credible to lenders and investors.

Like any savvy marketer, WISC has packaged its capabilities into a few service packages directed to specific needs of entrepreneurs and inventors.

- New Product Development Assessment
- Competitive Intelligence Report
- Customer Assessment

- Distributor Assessment
- Product Licensing Partner Search

The "umbrella service" is the **New Product Development Assessment**. This combines a technical feasibility estimate, an assessment of competition, a preliminary patent search, plus an estimate of market demand and market trends. The price is $895. For a physical product, have a prototype available.

You may decide to have WISC do deeper analysis of selected issues after reviewing the findings in the New Product Development Assessment. This work is customized for your needs, so there is no fixed price.

In the **Competitive Intelligence Report**, you'll work with WISC to identify the types of potential competitors. Then WISC researches databases to identify companies fitting your criteria. WISC works with you to develop a questionnaire, and then conducts phone interviews with all the selected companies (20 or more). WISC assesses the results with industry experts, and prepares a competitor matrix. The summary report includes suggested next steps.

In the **Customer or Market Assessment**, you'll work with WISC to identify potential customers and develop an interview questionnaire. WISC conducts the survey and summarizes results into a report you can use to modify your product or marketing plans, from positioning to pricing to promotion.

In the **Distributor Assessment**, you work with WISC to identify potential distributors and prepare an interview questionnaire.

WISC conducts the survey and summarizes the findings. You can use this to validate your sales forecast, logistics, and pricing.

In a **Product Licensing Partner Search**, you work with WISC to identify potential licensors and develop a survey as above. WISC conducts the survey and summarizes results. WISC may also develop and carry out a 30–90 day plan to decide if a licensing strategy is right for your product.

You decide what you need and when you need it. WISC provides the expertise to find the players and interview them. Together you figure out how to use the findings.

Low cost advice can be an eye-opener without breaking the bank! "Research Reduces Risk," and that's why it adds credibility at the same time. Check out WISC to get real world direction for your new product design and marketing.

6.6 Summary of Revenue Growth Techniques

Every business wants to grow, and that means grow profits. Maybe we want to change the world as well, or at least make it better, but even then we need profit to keep doing so. More profit is better! Here is a summary of prior articles examining techniques for growth. Which ones work best for you?

1. **Profit Assessment: Is My Business Worth Doing?**

   How much are you putting into your business, and what are you getting out of it in return? Could you get the same profit from another activity with less effort or risk? Design your business to generate a 20% annual return on the money you invested and borrowed.

2. **The Business Growth Machine**

   Imagine yourself as the operator of a business growth machine, with dials to show changes in key business results, and lots of levers that enable you to cause those changes. You are the "great and powerful Oz"—the small business owner! Which levers should you pull first, and when will the results change?

3. **Business Growth Techniques: Fast or Slow**

   As you decide which lever to use to grow your business, you'll be thinking about what could go wrong as well as dreaming about success. You want some noticeable gains soon. You don't want a major effort for a minor or temporary gain. You don't want a major risk if smaller steps can deliver the same value.

4. **Grow Quick with "Quick Wins"**

   The ideal business growth project delivers higher cash flow within 30 days. The increase is sustainable for months to come, it can be done within current resources, and you can stop it easily if it does not work out. If it's ideal, it also generates more customer loyalty and better employee morale. Does that sound like heaven on earth? It's a *quick win*. Where can you find one?

5. **Grow Pretty Fast with Current Customers**

   Why are current customers a "pretty fast" growth opportunity? You know how to reach them, and you can be fairly sure they will pay attention when you communicate. You know what products, features, and services they like. You know where they like to buy, and how much they normally spend. More knowns means less risk, and less time required for trial and error marketing. Your relationship with these customers offers more "control" than trying to reach new customers.

6. **Serious Growth Efforts: To Attract New Customers, Change Something!**

   Attracting new customers in your same target market is not just a communications challenge. A little "reinventing yourself" is needed! After all, you've been operating in their neighborhood for years, but they haven't chosen you! Why not? How are they meeting their needs without you? Did your message not reach them, or did they hear it but decide not to be interested?

7. **Serious Growth: How to Choose a New Target Segment**

   Attracting new customers in your current geographic market need not be "more of the same." You can expand your customer base by appealing to customer groups who did not realize your product could be their solution. Such a group is called a "market segment," a group of potential customers who all face the same need. Identify promising segments by imagining your product solving different needs.

8. **Growing through New Distributors and Collectors**

   You can interpret the word distributor more broadly than its traditional meaning. You are looking for situations where you can build *one* relationship to generate *multiple* customers. Imagine you are seeking "collectors."

9. **Major Growth Effort: Choosing and Entering a New Geographic Market**

   New markets and new products are major growth efforts. Which do you think is easier: entering a new market like the one you are serving today, or developing and introducing a new product to your current market? New similar markets are easier than new product introductions because you already have a successful recipe for your market. Now you can grow by replicating it where conditions are similar. Replicating is easier than creating!

10. **Major Growth Effort: New Product**

    If you are doing more than merely adding a flavor or a feature to current products, new product development is probably the most complex growth activity you can find. Why? Because you are re-assessing everything that makes your company work, and changing many parts of it. You'll certainly change marketing, operations, and supply chain. You might also change organization, technology platform, and financing. Complexity takes time and adds risk. To increase chances for success, the business must reduce complexity, so introduce the new product first to your *current* geographic market. The risk is reduced even further if the target is your current customers rather than a new segment of your home market.

Your business growth machine has many levers. For revenue growth, start with "quick wins," then develop more revenue from current customers. To attract new customers, target a new segment and change something! Develop relationships with distributors and "collectors." When moving to new markets, find similar areas, and grow in concentric circles. New products can be the most complex effort, so use a defined process to select the best ideas, focus your resources, test frequently, and don't be afraid to say "no go!"

Growing through Operations

Growing through Operations

OPERATIONS ARE THE FOUNDATION OF THE BUSINESS. Since growth requires a firm foundation, you'll want to improve your operations before major expansion moves. The good news is that improving operations involves less risk than growing revenue, and the results happen much faster. Why? Because the owner has more control over operations than over the decisions of potential customers. The payoffs in efficiency and quality boost revenues, reduce costs, and raise profits. What else is there?

Part Three Driving Concepts

- Improve operations by revising processes to remove the eight types of waste: overproduction, inventory, waiting time, transportation, over-processing, motion, defects, and under-utilization.

- Many signals of waste are visible to the experienced analyst. Finding opportunities for process improvement is never difficult!

- The process improvement effort starts with process mapping. In addition to the value of the improved process, this effort has other important dividends. It bonds team members together and boosts their motivation as well.

- There is a toolbox of proven process improvement techniques. Choose the tools that will matter most to your business.

- The two most important costs for most businesses are labor and materials. Labor efficiency depends on employee performance and process improvement. Material efficiency is determined by the design and purchasing processes.

Techniques Presented in Part Three

Topic	Technique	Content	Articles
Improving Operations	Improve Operations before expanding	Operations improvement allows more control, hence less risk than revenue growth levers. Growth requires a solid foundation in efficient operations.	7.1
	Finding Operations Opportunities	Look for the eight wastes, using signals from operations, purchasing, and management.	7.2
	Process Mapping	Assemble a team, develop SIPOC, observe, map with post-it notes. Questions to trigger improvement ideas. Estimate value and plan implementation.	7.3, 7.4
	Simple techniques to remove waste	Seven principles and 30 techniques.	7.5
	Tips to manage Labor and Material Costs	Measure and manage non-productive time. Recover its cost in pricing. Five tips to improve purchasing.	7.6

Chapter 7: Improving Operations

7.1 Improving Operations: The Low-Risk Path to Growing Profits

Is your business a "fixer-upper?" Success depends on a solid foundation, whether you are building a house or building a business. You wouldn't build another level on a crumbling foundation, and you shouldn't try to grow a business with fundamental weaknesses. The foundation of the business is Operations—the way you use resources to add value to raw materials so that customers want to buy the output.

In terms of the "The Business Growth Machine" introduced in Chapter 4, this means you should work on the Cost Control levers before the Revenue Growth Levers.

Cost Control Levers	
Variable Cost	**Fixed Cost**
• Labor hours	• % nonproductive labor
• Labor wages	• Rent
• Labor benefits	• Marketing
• Material amount	• Office supplies/misc.
• Material cost	• Your salary/benefits
• Subcontractors	• Professional services*
• Shipping	• IT systems
• Sales commission	• Interest
	• More!

*Professional services includes consultants, lawyer, accountant, other outside services

Cost control, along with quality, is how we measure operational success. Revenue Growth and Cost Control can both improve profits, but you have more control over improving your own operations than growing sales. You know your operations and your people, but growing sales depends the unknown—the decisions of potential customers you have not yet been able to attract.

Starting your growth efforts with improving operations makes sense for two reasons:

- More control means less risk, so forecasted results are much more likely to actually happen with cost control than with revenue growth initiatives.

* Revenue growth moves will have a higher payoff if they are based on excellent rather than weak operations.

For example, if 25% of the units produced by ABC Widget Company need "rework" to fix quality problems, adding more sales results in more rework. But if ABC can reduce rework to 5%, its sales growth will result in much greater profit growth.

Finding Opportunities: What Needs Improvement?

How do you spot the signals showing opportunities for improvement? Every business has these signals, but owners usually overlook them as they focus on day to day tasks. You need a frame of reference to know what to look for, and an outside perspective to know what level of performance is good. A consultant can offer both, based on broad experience analyzing many types of companies. The next article suggests what to look for.

How to Improve Operations

The goal of operations is high quality production based on efficient use of materials, machinery, and labor. Production is the output. Materials, machinery, and labor are the inputs. Productivity—the end result of cost control—is the value of the outputs divided by the cost of the inputs.

How do you improve operations to achieve better productivity? You use a combination of people management and process improvement.

People Management

Earlier articles explained how to motivate and train your workforce. Employees must *want* to do the right thing, *know how* to do it, and *know why* the right methods work best. See Chapters 1 and 3.

A well-managed workforce is the key to efficient and predictable production, and it's also the key to improving operations. Here's why. The best managers invite motivated, well-trained employees to participate in finding better production methods. These employees know the details, the opportunities, and the potential pitfalls you'll encounter in implementation. The opportunity to improve the design of their jobs strengthens their motivation even more, creating a virtuous circle—an upward spiral of continuous improvement.

Process Improvement Begins with Mapping a Business Process

A *business process* is the sequence of steps used to produce an output. Every business has several processes. Examples of "high level" processes include ordering supplies, producing widgets, quality control, billing and collection, hiring and training, and cash management. Most of these have sub-processes, such as accepting shipments, stocking and counting inventory, delivering it to work stations, and the various production steps.

Improving a process is the fundamental route to improving operations quality, cost control, and productivity. Process improvement is the *best* technique for profit improvement because it produces more profit with *every* sale, and it's under your control.

Process improvement generates more and more profit as the business grows because it controls variable costs, increasing the contribution or gross margin in both dollars and percentage of revenue. If fixed costs (overhead) stay the same, then this higher gross margin increases profit by the same amount.

To improve a process, you must understand how it works today. The tool is a process map—a special kind of flowchart. It's a visual method for showing the process in steps, crossing departmental boundaries and linking it to preceding and following processes. The best process maps show more than the physical output. They also show how long each step takes, who does them, and the paper or digital record produced.

Once you can see the process as it is today, you can also see how it might be changed. Your goal is *substantial change*, reducing cost or improving quality by as much as 50%. Following articles tell you what signals to look for, what questions to ask, and how to map and improve your processes, the surest way to grow profits.

7.2 Finding Opportunities for Operations Improvement

To make a diagnosis, doctors ask patients about their history and symptoms. They're looking for signals pointing to a problem. A ship's pilot looks for familiar landmarks to find the safe channel. A business analyst uses the same approach, looking for familiar signals to find improvement opportunities, based on experience in assessing many companies. The analyst starts with a set of questions.

When the analyst asks what you do, why you do it that way, and what you don't do, resist the natural tendency to be defensive! Remind yourself that every weakness today is an opportunity to improve quality and profits tomorrow. Rather than withholding information and rejecting new ideas, work with the analyst to seek out the signals to start your growth engine! You wouldn't withhold symptoms from the doctor, so don't hide signals from the analyst you hired to make your business healthy.

What to Look for: The Eight Wastes

Waste is any activity that absorbs resources but creates no value in the customer's eyes. You and the analyst will identify opportunities by examining your operations to find the Eight Wastes (*muda*) made famous by the Lean movement, based on the Toyota Production System.[21] They are:

1. **Overproduction:** Some steps or some entire processes produce more than is needed now; excess sits in inventory. The solution is small batch sizes, and quick set-up time between batches.

2. **Inventory:** This is money sitting idly, adding no value. It could be raw material, or partially completed production, or finished goods awaiting sale. The solution is ordering in small amounts ("just-in-time") while managing shipping costs, and processing in small batches to avoid stockpiling finished work. This requires good demand forecasts, and efficient setup routines.

3. **Waiting Time:** Work waits in queues if it is completed before the next step is ready to handle it. People wait for work (shifting to nonproductive tasks in the meantime) if the prior step takes longer than their step. Both types of waiting time make production slower, resulting in resources adding cost without adding value.

   Many solutions can be considered. The first is balancing the workflow, so all the steps take the same amount of time, called *takt* time. Another is eliminating handoffs, so there are fewer waiting queues. Quality initiatives can minimize rework, which makes all the downstream steps wait for nonproductive do-overs. Other solutions include shorter set-up time, parallel processing, and subassemblies.

4. **Transportation:** Time and effort spent moving materials, partially finished assemblies, and finished goods add no value to the finished product. These tasks delay finished goods and sales, tying up resources in the meantime.

   Solutions deal with logistics: locating production closer to markets, locating supplier and storage closer to production, shipping at night, receiving at night, and ordering with proper lead times.

5. **Over-Processing:** Avoid time and machine hours spent producing "bells and whistles" which add no value for customers, i.e., they do not enable a higher price. The solution lies in revising product design, especially any design element that requires use of a crucial or "bottleneck" machine also used for key production steps. You want to make sure the load on such machines is limited to only the essentials, since their availability determines your pace of output.

6. **Motion:** Time spent moving people or materials from one place to another within the production process adds no value in the customer's eyes. The solution can involve layout of the production facility's machinery and storage, assignment of tasks to workgroups, and finding faster ways to move.

7. **Defects:** Poor quality production results in wasted material (scrap), wasted labor hours for rework, and warranty costs. These not only waste resources themselves, but can slow the entire output cycle, delaying cash flow and making downstream resources less productive due to waiting time.

   Solutions involve standards and measurements, in-process inspection by the workers themselves, designing methods and tools that prevent mistakes (*poka-yoke*), holding each workgroup accountable for correcting its own mistakes, and incentives for achieving both quality *and* productivity targets together.

8. **Underutilizing Skills:** When people can do more than they are asked to do, the money spent on others doing that work is waste. The solution is to look to your own staff first. Recognize that one person can operate more than one machine, and fill more than one role. Consider work cells where one or more people handle a variety of tasks as a team. Challenge the team to invent new methods for significant change.

Keeping in mind the Eight Wastes, you and the analyst will look for signals that point to Waste, to find opportunities to remove it.

Operations Signals

- Piles of Work in Progress indicate an unbalanced production line, bottlenecks, and parts shortages. These can signal several types of waste, such as overproduction, waiting time, over-processing, defects, inventory, and wasted motion to move around the piles.

* Scrap, field failures, and warranty costs indicate defect wastes.

* Rework hours indicate defect wastes as well.

* Machine downtime can indicate wasted hours as employees wait for work.

* Uneven line speed is another indicator of employee waiting waste.

* People waiting for work, and work waiting for people.

* Absence of visual progress indicators hides quality and delay issues, resulting in waiting and defect wastes.

* Absence of standardization and measurements also hides quality and delay issues, and hampers improvement decisions.

* Employee workpaths, such as chasing parts and visually checking inventory before taking an order, can reveal inaccurate inventory waste as well as excess labor hours.

* Transport time and costs involve their own expense and delays.

* Excessive customizing suggests wastes such as over-processing and waiting.

* Absence of any recent 5S event suggests wasted inventory costs, potential safety issues, processing delays for finding the right tools, and wasted motion as workers move around barriers such as surplus materials and machines.

  o 5S stands for Sort, Straighten, Shine, Standardize, Sustain.[22] It is a Lean technique to transform a sloppy shop into a smooth-running machine by disposing of unnecessary supplies, tools, and equipment, while sorting the remainder into a clean layout that supports efficient production. The morale boost is an additional benefit!

Purchasing Signals

- Inventory turnover analysis assesses money tied up in unused materials and finished product. One benchmark is a two-week supply. Comparing your turnover to industry benchmarks reveals the waste.

- Absence of performance measurements for key suppliers suggests possible part shortages, quality issues, and even cash management problems.

- Absence of recent competitive bids indicates that material costs may be too high.

- Absence of outsourcing comparisons signals opportunities for process improvement and cost savings.

- Asset utilization measurements reveal bottlenecks and surplus, each representing their own types of waste.

Management Signals

- Absence of forecast vs. actual comparisons indicates potential for excessive inventory or staff, as well as cash flow issues.

- Absence of measurements on "% quotes accepted" can reveal pricing and differentiation problems, which can turn into wasted inventory and hours.

- Statistics on the timing and accuracy of invoices and payments can suggest problems in these processes. These can threaten cash flow, the lifeblood of the business.

- Absence of documentation for key processes, often due to over-reliance on the knowledge of a few key workers, creates greater risk if they leave, potential internal controls problems, and wasted opportunities to improve those processes.

- Weak internal controls create the risks of fraud and poor cash flow. Internal controls are methods to ensure the integrity of operational, financial, and accounting information. They also ensure that management policies are followed throughout the organization. One example of internal controls is the requirement that at least two employees are involved in every financial transaction.

- Distributed authority to reduce prices creates the risk of poor margins, damaging cash flow.

- Operating more than one IT system indicates unreliable information flow due to discrepancies between systems (e.g. inventory, variable cost, margin analysis). Wasted hours is one result.

7.3 The Process Mapping Conversation— Getting Started

"A picture is worth 10,000 words."[23] The visual nature of a process map makes it understandable. Once employees can see the process laid out in steps, they can start communicating with each other about their experience with it and their ideas to make it better.

A team of employees creates a preliminary high level view called SIPOC (see below), and then uses observations to create a first draft process map. Then team members improve the first draft by adding decision points, customizing steps, rework loops, response to shortages of parts, and pursuit of approvals. At the same time, they'll ask aloud "Why do we do it that way? What if we did this activity differently?"

Developing the process map as a team triggers discussion of ways to improve the business. This interaction is a major benefit of process mapping, in addition to the process improvements themselves.

Google offers plenty of examples of process maps. At least one has an embedded video showing the development of a process map for peanut butter and jelly sandwiches![24] Slideshare is a good source as well.[25] A good tutorial on process mapping can be found at *Balanced Scorecard's "Handbook for Basic Process Improvement,"*[26] especially pages 21–24 in the PDF page count.

In keeping with our focus on techniques, this article and the next will focus on the step by step process for building a process map and seeking ways to improve it, with an emphasis on the value of the conversation along the way.

Step 1: Choose a Process
Make a list of the "high level" processes that define your business. A previous article offered some examples, such as ordering, production, invoicing, receiving, and inventory management. Choose one, or a sub-process within the high level process, where changes could offer major impact on quality and productivity.

After you have worked through one process, you can repeat the effort for a different process later.

Decide how to measure success in the chosen process, e.g. widgets per hours (or hours per widget) with x level of quality. What level of performance does the current process deliver, specifically, in numbers?

Next, how much improvement is your goal? It should be major. Maybe a 50% improvement?

Step 2: Assemble the Team, Define the Rules, Develop the SIPOC

The team should not exceed five to seven people. They must be knowledgeable about the process. All the departments with a major role in the process should be represented. Appoint a team leader, whose job is to manage progress and team dynamics, and keep bosses informed. The leader's job is to foster the conversation, *not* to insist on their own view of the right answer!

Team rules include the target completion date, how much time they will spend per day or week, their authority to arrange tests of improvements, and approval of any resources they will need. Rules also include expectations on meeting preparation and behavior.

SIPOC is a summary view of the process at a very high level. The acronym stands for Supplier, Input, Process, Output, Customer. As you can see, the name is the sequence for adding value. Here's an example for Car Repair:[27]

Supplier	Input	Process	Output	Customer
– Vehicle owner – Customer service representative – Facility manager – Parts window	– Repair inquiry – Vehicle for repair – Permission to proceed with individual recommendations – Open bay – Parts for approved repairs – Observations	– Schedule visit – Diagnose problem – Prepare work order – Source parts – Perform repairs – Notify that service is complete	– Appointment date and time – Repair recommendations and cost estimates – Work order – Parts for approved repairs – Telephone/e-mail/text message notification – Repaired vehicle	– Vehicle owner – Mechanic – Customer service representative

A more complete example would also show completion time targets and other "critical to quality" requirements for each input and output. Later, the employee team's process map will add detail to every entry on the SIPOC.

Step 3: Observe the Current Process

The team must fully understand the process before trying to change it, to avoid creating problems rather than solutions! Understanding starts with observation (usually several times) and recording what they saw, in detail. It helps if they know what to look for! They should try to answer these questions:

- What inputs are needed, and how are they gathered, by who, when?

- What are the processing actions taken, decisions, inspections, and approvals?

- Again who does these, when, and how long do they take?

- What are the exceptions, and how are they handled?

- What documents are produced or updated, and what is done with them?

The team will take pains to record what really happens rather than what is supposed to happen! They will focus on activities in all the involved departments, especially on handoffs from one department to another.

The Extra Dividend
You know the team will already be trading ideas for doing things better, even before they create the first draft of the process map. How valuable is that interest and engagement?

7.4 The Process Mapping Conversation— Seeking Improvements

The excitement starts for the team once they've collected their observations to show how the process is actually done today. Listen to their buzz—that's the sound of creativity, teamwork, and engagement. It's the sound of motivated employees!

Step 4: Map the Current Process
Gather the observed information. Write the major elements of the process on post-it notes (because they can be moved around easily) and put them on the wall in order, so the entire team can see them at once.

Then insert components (on post-it notes) under each of the major elements. These are decisions, inspections, rework loops, approvals, record-making, and sub-processes used to create inputs or specialized steps. Some of these sub-processes will be important enough to require their own process maps.

The second level of analysis puts all these post-it notes in order, showing the sequence in which they happened. Now you have a high level map.

Like any early mapmaker, you will see areas of unknowns. Some may be important enough to fill in based on further observation. After adding these post-it notes in another meeting, you'll have a mid-level version of the map. Test this version by reviewing it with those who do the work, and insert their corrections.

Step 5: Analyze the Map for Possible Improvements

The goal here is to simplify the process (and the process map) by identifying wasted time and effort. Some questions like these may trigger important ideas:

- What would happen if this step were eliminated? Are any steps redundant?

- Can rules such as approval levels be changed to make any steps unnecessary?

- Can visual signals be introduced to avoid delays or smooth the flow of priority tasks?

- Can some steps be done in parallel rather than waiting for completion of a previous step, such as using subassemblies?

- Is the step being done by the right person?

- Is the step a work-around due to poor training or parts shortages?

* Is the step a rework loop? How can you eliminate the need for it?

* Does the step add value to the product or service in the customer's eyes? If not, what would be the result of eliminating it?

* If more work was added to one step, would that eliminate a subsequent step and save time overall?

* Which steps seem to have the greatest impact on cycle time? Do we need to know more details about them to make them more productive?

* Do current computer systems have unused functions that could be "turned on" to replace time spent on record production, gathering inputs, or production steps?

* How could we use a wireless computer (e.g. tablet) to speed up some steps?

Step 6: Estimate the Value per Improvement, and Collect Data to Verify Estimates

The team is not finished until it can predict the value of its changes—do they deliver the target level of improvement on the chosen measurements?

Significant changes must be tested in operation, observed, and measured for their impact and unintended consequences. Predictions without verification aren't worth much more than telling you what to test.

The testing effort also helps clarify how implementation should be done. The team's final recommendation will include proposed process changes, measured effect, implementation plan, and timeline. The implementation plan must consider communication, training, job aids, measurements, and incentives, i.e., all the aspects of setting your employees up for success (Article 3.4).

The Extra Dividend is the Conversation

You went through a few weeks of extra effort, and what did you get from it? What value was added?

- You understand a key business process better than ever before.

- Your employees found improvements that will boost quality (sales) and productivity (profits).

- Your employees were honored by your trust in their judgment; their motivation has never been higher.

- Your employees began to think like an owner, which promises more improvements both in their daily work and when you analyze the next process.

- Your employees developed better team spirit from working together on an exciting project.

So what do you think? Does it seem worthwhile to map and improve a key process? Are you or they working on anything more important right now?

7.5 Simple Techniques for Removing Waste from Processes

Robots are not the answer for small business! To produce value at optimal cost, small businesses need simple techniques, not expensive robots and complex MRP systems. Your processes should be able to produce a high variety of outputs at high quality levels with fast cycle time, low operating cost, low inventory, and good information flow.

Start with understanding your process today, displaying it on a process map. In the book *Lean Thinking*, Womack and Jones described the mindset for process mapping this way: "Can you put yourself in the position of a *design* as it progresses from concept to launch, an *order* as information flows from initial request to delivered product, and a *physical product* as it progresses from raw material to the customer, and describe what will happen to you each step along the way?"[28]

Process Design Principles

1. **Standardize**: Define how your process *should* work, and how you measure whether it does, at each step along the way. Standards enable a common assessment, a common understanding of success, and a shared basis for analysis.

2. **Simplify**: Shorten the flow so less can go wrong. Remove steps that add no value. You could eliminate them or move them out of the critical path with work cells or subassemblies. You could also shift tasks to other steps, or to the customer, supplier, or outsourcer.

3. **Balance the Steps**: Organize your process into major steps so that each requires the same time interval (called *takt* time by Toyota). This enables work to flow through the process at a continuous pace, without wasting time in queues waiting to be processed.

4. Use a **pull system** to obtain **continuous flow**: Each work step pulls what it needs from the prior step "just in time." You don't order or produce large quantities that wait for subsequent processing. Instead, each step produces only small buffer quantities, not mountains of "work in progress." Continuous flow is the opposite of "batch and queue."

5. **Visual Alerts**: Design visual signals for monitoring progress, prioritizing work, triggering the pull (and ordering) of inputs, and displaying incomplete sets of parts ("kitting"). Visual signals enable quicker response than burying these key measures and events in expensive information systems.

6. **Find and Optimize the Bottleneck**: Identify the one process step that determines the pace for the entire process. Focus on improving its throughput to drive the productivity of the entire process. See below for tactics. Once you improve the bottleneck, rebalance the steps for a faster cycle time, and look for the next bottleneck.

7. **Continuous Improvement** (*kaizen* in Japanese): Improving one process affects other processes. Modify them, and then return to the first one to improve it further. This yields constant gains in productivity and profits, rather than delaying benefits by waiting for the perfect overall solution before implementing.

Some Simple Techniques to Implement the Principles

Standardize	— Establish time, volume, and quality metrics for key steps; these enable workers to inspect the quality of their own work. Monitor results per person and per product. Investigate and correct shortfalls. — Rejects must be corrected by the group who produced them. — Design work processes and tools so they can be used only in the right way (mistake-proof, or *poka-yoke*), e.g., tabs on jigs or edits to prevent input errors.
Simplify	— Create subassemblies removed from the main flow. — Condense work steps or subassemblies so several are done by a single person or work cell. This removes handoffs, which often result in batch-and-queue delays. — Use your computer system rather than manual records for recording and storing information about process flow and task completion. — Limit options offered; customization is inefficient unless it comes with a high enough price premium. — Look for ways to offload tasks. Consider whether customers or suppliers can perform some inputs themselves. — Periodically assess outsourcing alternatives for non-core tasks and processes.
Balance the Steps	— Reorganize tasks into equal-length work steps. — Use work cells and subassemblies. — Recognize that one worker can operate more than one machine. — Prescribe and limit the size of buffer stocks.
Pull and Continuous Flow	— Prevent overproduction in any one work step by triggering replenishment of the buffer stock via a signal from the following work step. — One example is a colored card (*kanban*) placed within the buffer stock so that it is exposed when the stock is low enough that replenishment is needed.
Visual Alerts	— *Kanban* is one form of visual alert. — Another is kitting: making a box with a shaped spot for each part in a set to be delivered to a work operation, to reveal when the part is missing. — Colored flags can show roaming supervisors whether a work step's progress is in danger of missing its time target. — Jobs waiting for Bottleneck processing can be marked with colored tags to show priority for customer due dates.

Optimize the Bottleneck	— Offload work by (1) re-examining product design to avoid the need for the bottleneck processing, (2) outsourcing, and (3) inspecting for rejects before they reach bottleneck processing. — Minimize bottleneck downtime by scheduling operators and maintenance. — Maximize bottleneck throughput by adding more capacity such as a bigger machine. — Optimize its flexibility to adjust to shifting priorities by organizing the work in small lots and streamlining setup routines. — Improve the operations *within* the bottleneck step. — Place the bottleneck as late in the production process as possible.
Continuous Improvement	— Implement improvements quickly to gain immediate payoffs. Just as small lot sizes improve efficiency, small improvement steps improve quality and profits. — Plan for a series of process improvement efforts. — Reflect on newly-learned methods and expertise, and standardize them so the same type of gains can be applied to other processes more quickly.

This article draws on "Lean" techniques based on the Toyota Production System, and the Theory of Constraints first demonstrated in Eliyahu Goldratt's *The Goal*. GE's famous Six Sigma methods support these approaches by stressing measurements and analysis techniques at each step of the analysis and improvement effort.[29]

Creativity in Process Improvement

Operations people often have limited opportunities to use their natural human creativity at work. So when they have the opportunity to use their creative ability to map a process and then improve it, the employees enjoy the change, and appreciate the owner's trust and respect for their abilities. They get great satisfaction from designing improvements, and go beyond the norm in their efforts for successful implementation.

Employee motivation, teamwork, and satisfaction all get a boost, at the same time company quality and profits grow. Use their creativity! It will be one of your best investments.

7.6 Tips on Labor and Material Cost Levers

Labor and material costs are worth examining closely. Each can amount to 20–25% of revenue, or run much higher depending on the type of business. In total, they can amount to 40 to 50% of revenue. They are the major elements in variable costs, and thus (together with price) determine the product and business margin.

Tips on Labor Cost

Employees are a critical resource for adding value to the finished product, so we are looking for ways to remove only *wasted* labor cost, not all labor cost! Three factors drive labor cost:

- Efficiency of productive time: previous articles show how to reduce production hours that add no value to the finished product, such as waiting within the process, rework, chasing parts, and moving material.

- Non-productive time: hours devoted to tasks that do not produce the product, such as training, setup time, cleaning, maintenance, paid absence, and other miscellaneous tasks.

- Cost per labor hour: pay rates, overtime, commissions, and benefits.

Non-productive Time

We humans never spend 100% of our time being productive. We take breaks, get paid time off, spend time learning and planning and getting ready to work, and keep records and maintenance up-to-date. None of these directly add value to the product in the customer's eyes. They may *enable* value-adding behaviors, but they don't add value themselves.

In a good operation, about 20% of paid time is nonproductive. If it is 40% in your operation, you need to make some changes. Do you know what that percentage is?

Why does it matter? It's important to recognize and measure the difference between productive and nonproductive hours when setting your prices. The common mistake is setting a price based on the variable labor hours/cost, which is job-dependent and 100% productive, but forgetting to count employee nonproductive hours as part of overhead. Your price must recover those costs too, or you will miss your profit target.

The technique is to show each type of labor (and payroll taxes) separately in your P&L or income statement. This way, when you develop your price quote by using a multiplier of wages ("shop rate") to cover overhead and target profit, the nonproductive labor cost is already included in the overhead. Accountants and software (e.g., QuickBooks) will not do this without special instructions. They like to treat all labor as a variable cost, which overstates your cost of production, or treat all labor as a fixed cost, which understates the production cost.

Hourly Labor Cost

Wages should be competitive in the market. If they are, there are still several tools to control labor cost.

- Incentives should be a high percentage of a competitive compensation package, and they should be paid only when both quality and productivity minimums are met.

- Benefits should match rather than exceed the market.

- Commissions should be higher for selling high margin products, and lower for low margin products.

- The cost of new recruits (hiring, training, and low productivity) must be considered when deciding how to handle fluctuations in demand.

- Overtime is usually cheaper than using subcontractors with similar pay scales. Why? Overtime does not change your benefits or fixed costs much, but the full impact of those costs are built into subcontractor fees, along with their profit margin.

- However, overtime should be limited to 20% of regular hours to minimize quality problems, declining productivity due to fatigue, and employee turnover.

- Unfortunately, the extra pay for overtime can be an incentive to reduce regular productivity, making proper performance standards and rewards even more important.

Tips on Material Costs

You want to avoid *excess* material costs. You want enough material with the right quality at just the right time for the best price. Your enemy in this effort is complacency: acceptance that the status quo is good enough, without trying to find better alternatives. Here are some improvement techniques:

- Keep statistics on supplier performance: timely delivery, percent rejects, and your satisfaction on special orders.

- Schedule supplier reviews, where you look at the marketplace to find other potential suppliers, and request bids to find the best offers. Do this every two or three years for your most important materials. One approach is to schedule one review. i.e., competitive bidding process, every six months.

- Negotiate *every* supplier offer. Offer a longer commitment, or choose a lower grade, or suggest less processing by the supplier to make it worth their agreement. It costs you nothing to ask. The only risk is that they say no!
    - It's worth doing! If you can cut your material cost by 10%, and material is 25% of revenue, that savings of 2.5% of revenue becomes a profit increase. If your profit is 15% of revenue and you grow it by 2.5 to 17.5%, you boost profits by 1/7 or 14%.
    - If your gross margin is 50% of revenue with material costs at 25% of revenue, negotiating supplier prices down by 10% reduces variable costs by 2.5%, increasing gross margin to 52.5%. In terms of profit as a percentage of revenue, this 2.5% margin gain is worth the same as growing sales by 5%. Which one is easier and more under your control?

- Review your replenishment order schedule to reduce inventory and improve cash flow. Forget the concept of "economic order quantity." Calculate how much safety stock you really need according to the supplier's best delivery interval and frequency. Then set up your internal "pull" signals to trigger a replenishment order when your safety stock reaches the minimum. Order just enough to tide you over until safety stock will reach that level again.

- Reconsider material storage. Find ways to store it near the operations that will use it. Make sure it's visible, not buried in a warehouse. This prevents wasted motion and the buildup of excess.

Fixed Cost Levers

Small business owners usually have a pretty good handle on their fixed costs such as rent, utilities, and professional services. However, some of these tips apply to fixed costs as well, such as periodically considering alternatives, negotiating prices, and minimizing usage.

Negotiating and Deciding

NEGOTIATING AND DECISION-MAKING TECHNIQUES are fundamental to all the growth levers: people management, revenue growth, operational excellence, and investment. Small business owners negotiate at all levels of the value chain, from suppliers to employees to distributors and customers.

Cash-starved small businesses have a smaller margin for error, so their decisions are more often critical to survival than in larger firms, yet small firms lack sophisticated decision support tools and access to high-priced expertise. No wonder owners sometimes agonize over how to grow! This part of the book offers some proven decision-making techniques to help overcome these hurdles.

Part Four Driving Concepts

- When you decide to negotiate, prepare with some research and reflection. Learn all you can about the topic and the other party. Figure out what they need (interest), not just what they might ask for (position). Decide your

BATNA—Best Alternative To Negotiated Agreement—in case talks fail, and decide your minimum threshold: the worst deal you would accept. Then anticipate the same two decisions for the other party.

- Plan your negotiating offers. Find some win/win solutions. Don't plan to convince the other party without changing something in your offer: choose the points you must have, and those you could give up. Consider style as well: how you're going deliver your message, and when, and how.

- Making decisions can be a major challenge for the owner of a small business. Delegate what you can to people closer to the situation. Get advice for the decisions you have to make.

- Use a Framework for making big decisions. This helps you think of creative alternatives, "outside the box."

- When assessing those alternatives, use some critical thinking. Accept that your information could be wrong, especially your assumptions about timing. Change some of the assumptions, and see if that would lead you to a different decision. Then turn to the judgment calls. Try to get to the bottom of your bias and advisors' bias. Change some of their assumptions and talk to those who disagree.

- Whatever decision you make will encounter resistance, and is likely to have ethical implications. Humility is the key ingredient here. Listen to others. Try to understand their point of view. See if you can tweak the plan to handle their needs and still get the outcome you need (or most of it). Deal with resistance in private.

Techniques Presented in Part Four

Topic	Technique	Content	Articles
Negotiating Skills	Research first	Know the topic, the other party, and two other suppliers. Choose your BATNA and threshold, and estimate the other's. Figure out their interest, often different from their position.	8.1
	Plan your solutions	Identify the decision-maker. Seek win/win. Respond off-target. Decide what to yield.	8.2
	Plan your behavior	Trading concessions. Who is first to mention price? Tone, listening, questions, non-verbal cues.	8.2
Decision-Making Skills	Making good decisions	Delegate; get advice.	9.1
	Use a Framework	How to use a 7 step approach.	9.2
	Assessing Alternatives	How to assess assumptions, advisor opinions, and your own. Change assumptions, find alternatives, and test.	9.3
	Dealing with Ethics and Resistance	Feel the impact on others, and use imagination to tweak for their benefit. Handle resistance privately, as a joint effort to improve the solution.	9.4
	Checklist for good decision-making	11 techniques.	9.5

Chapter 8: Negotiating Techniques

8.1 Knowledge Is Power: Five Ways to Win Negotiations before They Start

For a successful negotiator, the guiding motto is this: "If it's worth doing, it's worth planning." Winning negotiations is less about how you behave across the table, and more about research and preparation before you sit down.

The negotiation process begins long before the parties meet. It starts when one party decides they need something from the other, or that they might get a better deal than the current arrangement.

The first two phases are complete even before the two parties sit down to talk:

- Phase 1: "Can't we do better than this? How much better?"

- Phase 2: "We're supposed to meet with them next week. How should we play it?"

- Phase 3: "Good morning! I'm glad we're finally talking face to face about this issue."

This article is about Phase 1; the next article addresses Phases 2 and 3.

Winning negotiators depend on winning research. To choose their negotiating strategy, they seek answers in five areas.

1. Know the topic and the other negotiator.

Knowing the topic is not as simple as it sounds. You need to know the facts and context from four viewpoints: unbiased outsider; man-on-the-street (how media would report it); the other party's interpretation; your own perspective. Each viewpoint has different values and biases, supported by the value (non-neutral) words they choose to describe the situation.

Your knowledge should include assessments of the likelihood and risks of possible outcomes: "Will they really file that lawsuit? Could they win? What if they did?" Leave the rose-colored glasses at home! These assessments will guide your decisions on the positions you plan to take, a Phase 2 activity.

Knowing the other negotiator is obviously important, but the information might be hard to find. Social media and industry contacts can be good starting points. You want to know their career history, their biases, what they value, positions they took in other negotiations vs. final outcomes, and the importance of this negotiation on their reputation in their company. You would also like to know what kind of negotiating style to expect, and the limits of their decision authority.

2. Find two other suppliers who could meet your needs.

The other negotiator may be more accommodating if they realize you have other options. You will let them know, but first be sure the alternatives can really meet your needs.

3. Decide your BATNA and your threshold: the lowest offer you would accept.

These are your boundaries. BATNA stands for Best Alternative to Negotiated Agreement.[30] It means your course of action if these negotiations do *not* result in a deal meeting your minimum threshold. What will you do then? Negotiate with the other two potential suppliers? Change the design to avoid using this supplier?

Knowing your BATNA helps you measure the lowest acceptable offer, or "threshold." The threshold will be a deal worth slightly more than the BATNA. Having these two minimums in mind, you can develop several better positions prior to taking your seat at the negotiating table.

4. Understand the other party's real "interest"; it's likely to be different than their "position."

Their position is the set of terms/price they propose. Avoid limiting your thinking to merely modifying their package. Instead, research to understand what they really need: their interest. Do they need the corn, or only the cob? Rather than being stuck dealing with their difficult *position*, there are probably many ways to satisfy their *interest* and yours at the same time. Knowing their interest (and yours) lets your creativity find a win/win solution, so your win does not mean their loss.

5. Forecast the other negotiator's BATNA and threshold.

"What else could they do?" Put aside your arrogance and belief in your own wonderful company, and try to think like the other party. How would they assess their alternatives? Who are their other two potential suppliers or customers? How does the other party think those two companies compare to yours? How much more would they pay to use your company?

Is the answer the same when you replace the value words in your analysis with neutral words? Using value words is how we fool ourselves! For example, change "legacy systems" to "proven systems," or change "inconsistent" to "flexible."

These five findings simplify and focus your planning. They set the minimums, and guide you to solutions the other party is likely to accept.

8.2 Negotiating Tactics: Content and Style

Once you understand the issue, the other party, and your own BATNA and threshold, you can move into Phase 2 of the negotiating process:

- Phase 1: "Can't we do better than this? How much better?"

- Phase 2: "We're supposed to meet with them next week. How should we play it?"

- Phase 3: "Good morning! I'm glad we're finally talking face to face about this issue."

After the research phase, think of Phase 2 as *Content*: what you will negotiate on and for. You'll decide these before the negotiation starts.

Think of Phase 3 as *Style*: the way you behave during the discussion itself. Recognize that although you may plan such tactics, your behavior must adapt to conditions "on the fly." As the boxer Mike Tyson says, "Everybody has a plan 'til they get punched in the mouth!"[31] That's when you adapt!

Phase 2: Plan the Content of Your Negotiations

1. Do your best to make sure you are negotiating with the Decision-Maker. If not, after you make a compromise deal with the subordinate, you may end up making further concessions to satisfy their boss. Some bosses need to prove their worth by being "tougher" than their subordinate.

2. Design some win/win solutions, considering the interests (not positions) of both sides. Then you can plan to take positions where the compromises lead to these win/win outcomes. For you to win, the other side does not need to lose. The best outcomes satisfy both sides.

3. Plan "off-target" responses to expected proposals. Direct, adversarial responses do not move the process forward. They just force the other side to try harder to justify their position, making progress even more difficult. Instead, your response can suggest a changed basis, such as bundling commitments or orders, or revised timing. You veer away from the position the other party has staked out. You change the terms of the discussion, in search of an area of common interest: win/win.

4. Choose your crucial negotiating points, and be prepared to yield on others. When the other party says "no," research shows they subconsciously feel an obligation to say "yes" later. This means that yielding on some points can help you win acceptance on other points. See "Defend Your Research," *Harvard Business Review*, December 2013.

Phase 3: Style - Tips for Behavior in Discussions

1. Don't bid against yourself! When you propose a price or position, wait until the other side makes a change or concession before changing your offer. If they say, "That's too high," do not come back with a lower price. Instead, explain why that price is reasonable, and suggest a change in their specifications that might open the door to a lower price.

2. Be careful about which side mentions their price first. Some say you should try to make the other side be first to mention a price, because that becomes the basis for negotiation, and it may be more favorable than what you would have offered. Others say you should be the first to state a price, because you *want* to set the basis for price negotiations! If you want to specify the basis for price discussions, then be the first.

3. Keep the tone light. Not only is it more pleasant, but your good-natured style shows you don't need this deal, that you have other equally-attractive choices. The result could be a more accommodating person across the table.

4. Paraphrase what you heard them say or saw them feel, and invite correction. This avoids wasting time with

misunderstandings, and builds goodwill by being a visibly interested listener.

5. Ask open-ended questions. "Why do you say that" is not open-ended, because it forces the other party to defend a statement or position. This makes it harder for them to back away from that position later. Instead, ask questions like "help me understand something better" or "tell me more about . . ."

6. Non-verbal cues can be a less adversarial way to get your message across.
   - Silence creates discomfort, so the other party will often fill the silence by saying more, revealing more about their interest.
   - Delay can make the other party anxious about unknown developments or overtures from your alternative suppliers. Their response is to become more flexible in what they'll agree to.
   - Other signals to make the other party doubt the strength of their position: arriving late, taking phone calls during the meeting, closing a portfolio, not taking notes, stepping out to discuss with colleagues, and any number of others.

This planning and behavior can get you where you want to go: an outcome that satisfies your interest. Your behavior need not be bombastic or cruel. Research enough to know the other party's interest, develop win/win solutions to satisfy their interest as well as your own, and negotiate off-target by changing the basis of discussion without directly opposing the proposals of the other side.

Chapter 9: Decision-Making Techniques

9.1 Making Good Decisions in a Small Business

Small business owners face decisions every day. They balance opportunity vs. risk, people effects vs. financial effects, and timing: do-it-now vs. later-is-better. Even deciding to do nothing different can be a fateful decision (or non-decision). Some examples of small business decisions:

How to do marketing?	Move to new location?	Grant customer request?
Buy new software?	What price to charge?	Modify employee schedule?
Make process changes?	Should I hire her or fire him?	Invest more capital?
Launch new product?	What components to make vs. buy?	Borrow money?

Decision-making is worth special attention because it has great impact and it's hard to do well consistently. Why is it hard?

- You never know all you need to know.

- Time is not your friend; often, you need to decide before you want to.

- If you get advice, it is divided, or based on poor understanding of your business.

- You expect resistance from key people: employees, customers, lenders.

- You don't like the impact on others; there may be ethical issues with no good solution.

- Due to the impact, you are afraid to make a mistake, so you delay. When you delay, the situation changes, and often you are left with fewer and less attractive options.

Take heart! There are some techniques—some ways to go about decision-making—that can result in better decisions and less risk.

First, Let Your People Decide for Themselves— Delegate for "Dynamic Decision-Making"

Too often a small business owner makes all the decisions for the firm. You have competent people. Why not use their brains? Large organizations cannot escalate all decisions to the top, so they had to develop a technique to make sure only the most critical decisions come to top management. You can do this too!

Delegate some authority to your people. Let them decide what to do. Train them well, make the processes clear, and then turn them loose *within limits*. Larger organizations call these limits a "**schedule of authority.**" This is a company policy set up as table, specifying the decision-making limits for each position or level. For example, frontline people can approve a refund up to $x, or buy supplies up to $y. Their supervisors have higher dollar limits. Maybe supervisors can also hire, or suspend but not fire, etc.

You will monitor the quality of their decisions, coaching them or changing the limits as needed. The result will be faster decisions with better consideration of the facts of the moment ("dynamic"), and a happier work force as well. For more on the benefits of delegating, see Article 3.3.

Second, Get Some Other Viewpoints

Being the decision-maker still leaves room for getting advice! And getting advice does not mean you are stepping back and letting your advisors decide. Advisors can include a partner, another business owner, a lawyer or accountant, a consultant, a key employee, a key customer, a friend, etc. Two advisors are better than one!

Here is what's good about getting advice:

* The advisor may know of examples where similar approaches were tried, and their results.

* The advisor may understand the implementation requirements of a particular choice better than you.

* The advisor will question things you take for granted.

* The advisor may have different biases than you, and less emotion, resulting in a more balanced approach.

- Explaining the situation to an advisor helps you explain it to yourself, organizing your thoughts and making your assumptions clear.

- The advisor may think of alternatives or impacts you missed.

- The advisor may know how to estimate or measure impacts better than you do, helping you to evaluate one alternative vs. another.

The next few articles will explain an overall approach for analyzing a situation, and then suggest techniques to use at each stage of the analysis.

9.2 A Framework for Making Decisions

Someone once asked a business owner, "Do you have trouble making decisions?" He answered, "Well, yes and no."

Making decisions is hard because life is complicated. It's hard to sort out all the considerations and give them proper weight. So here is an approach that helps you sort everything out. Good decisions are more likely when your thinking follows these steps:

1. Define the Problem.

2. List Key Background Information, including all the numbers that may help you weigh impact and compare alternatives. Use "value-neutral" words. You may need 15–20 bullet points.

3. Solution Criteria: Not the solution itself, but what the right solution must accomplish. Usually there will be two or three measurable developments. Any alternative

course of action that does not accomplish these measurements does not solve the problem, and thus can be rejected.

4. Key Questions: What you would like to know to help you choose the right course of action?

5. Three Alternative Courses of Action (or more, not less), with pros and cons for each.

6. Recommended Solution: may be a blend of two or more "alternative courses of action."

7. Describe the Implementation Requirements.

Here are some tips on how to use each step.

1. Define the Problem

You want to find the underlying issue, not just the symptom. To be sure you've gotten to the real issue, ask WHY as many as five times.

For example, too many of the people I hire quit after a few months. Why do they do that? They feel pressured because their performance is criticized. Why is their performance criticized? Because it falls short of our standards. Why does it fall short? Do they know what the standard is, and why it's necessary? Do they have adequate training? Did you verify they understood the training and could perform the task? If yes, then why aren't they performing the task well now? Do you use incentives, and do they motivate the right or the wrong behavior? Are there implicit rewards that motivate them to skip steps in task performance? Can you change those?

This multi-level thought process takes you from solving "feeling pressured" to fixing the rewards, or it might lead you to fixing the training. If the underlying problem is rewards or training, relaxing pressure would not solve the problem. So it's crucial to carefully define the problem you must solve.

2. List Key Background Information

This step is an attempt to boil down the welter of information and emotion into just the relevant facts and expectations, so you can focus on what matters most. To make it quick, use bullet items rather than paragraphs. Examples include:

- Describe the market and your position in it.

- Describe the assets you or your business have, and why they are relevant.

- What do customers value, and how does your offer compare to competing offers for those value elements, also called "buying criteria"?

- Who is involved and how?

- What are the current performance measurements, what are the targets for them, and what are your actual results?

- What are the important cost elements and the cost of each?

- What would it take to make this change or that change: skills, cost, time?

- What would be the effects of each of these changes?

- Why haven't you made these changes before now?

- When do you need to change something, and why then?

- What happens if you change nothing?

Be sure to include all the numbers that can be relevant to your decision. As noted above, you might use 15 to 20 bullet items to cover the relevant information for making a decision.

Consider bias when you make this list. When you select information, you are excluding some other information. Would another reasonable person mention something here that you have not? Why did you exclude it? Should you reconsider?

One dangerous tendency is describing the facts with value-laden words. These are usually adjectives, like mere, trivial, huge, frightening, foolish, etc. Reconsider your list and edit it to use only value-neutral words. This removes distracting emotions. Instead, just cite numbers (not adjectives) to communicate size or impact. If you are not sure of the numbers, make an assumption and note that it should be tested later. Use numbers rather than adjectives to tell the story. In this section of the Framework, your goal is to list the relevant facts, not evaluate them.

3. Identify the Solution Criteria

Solution criteria are the measurements showing that the solution—whatever it is—has solved the problem. Criteria might be: sales or profits meet target; employee loss rate changes from x to y; percent rejects falls from a to b; or the customer satisfaction survey's "completely satisfied" category rises from c to d.

Use these solution criteria as tests when considering alternative courses of action (solutions). If that course is not likely to result in the desired criteria (changes in measurements), then it must be rejected as not solving the problem.

4. Key Questions

These three to five questions are inspired by the solution criteria and background. They will lead you to possible courses of action, i.e. they help you brainstorm. Examples might be:

- How can we increase sales by x amount by y date?

- How will competitors react?

- How will we get the skills to build a web presence?

- Is our facility big enough to handle the necessary increase in sales?

- Can we find a faster machine? How can we afford it?

- What are the alternatives to a particularly troublesome step in our production process?

5. Select at least Three Alternative Courses of Action, with pros and cons for each

This step is crucial. Its goal is to stop the normal tendency to consider only one answer, or to set up the problem as a choice between two approaches. Research confirms that by casting a wider net, you broaden your thinking and end up with a better overall recommendation.[32]

For example, if the problem is growth, some alternatives might be: change the product; change the price; change the marketing; motivate the sales force. In each case, when saying what the alternative is, say *how* you would do it so you know what to evaluate. How would the product change? What would be the new pricing structure? What kind of new marketing approach? What kind of new motivation system?

You can get to this point in the Framework in 30 minutes! Then you need to *analyze* the pros and cons, which you selected based on intuition, to measure their impact. A spreadsheet to compare alternative financials may be useful here. You may also want to assign weighting factors to various pros and cons, because some are more important or have more impact than others.

Now is the time to review all this thinking with others. You may find they suggest different alternatives and different pros and cons, or they may weigh the importance of pros and cons differently. They may also suggest low-risk ways to test your assessments of pros and cons, to be sure of your measurements of impact.

6. Recommendation

Here is where you make your preliminary decision on what to do and how to do it. The best solutions are often blends of two or more alternative courses, with staged implementation to allow adjustments based on findings as you proceed.

7. Implementation Requirements

A solution that cannot be implemented successfully is not a solution at all! In this final step you list the sequence of implementation activities, and reassess for practicality. This can cause you to change your recommendation, or its staging. Once the implementation requirements are clear and reasonable, you can start work on making them happen, using a project plan to keep yourself on track. Implementation is where good decisions usually come apart, and fail to deliver the solution criteria! Paraphrasing Edison, solutions are 10% inspiration and 90% perspiration!

9.3 Decision-Making: Assessing Alternatives

If you defined the problem correctly and created several alternative courses of action, you're on the road to success! But that was the easy part! Assessing alternatives is the hardest part of decision-making. It depends on judgment, sorting out bias, and testing your intuition. You ask yourself:

- Is my information (i.e. "background") correct? Can I get more information to test assumptions?

- How do I use or weigh this information, and the advice of others, to choose the best alternative?

- Have I considered ethics in choosing my preferred alternative?

- How do I deal with resistance from employees and other stakeholders?

This article addresses the first two: information and judgment. The next article deals with ethics and resistance.

Is My Information Correct?

You will never have all the information you would like, but you may have enough information to decide. However, the information you already have may be wrong, or inapplicable. And you may be able to get more of the missing information you would like to have.

In the Background section of your Framework, you listed the numbers you thought were relevant to solving the problem. Before deciding, look again at those numbers. Who developed them, from what sources? Did they make some assumptions? Of course they did! Examine those assumptions:

* Are they based on the same type of situation you are facing: the same customers, competitors, technology, etc.? If not, can you or someone else suggest a better basis?

* How likely is the trend they assumed? Is a different trend equally likely? If it is, use the different trend to develop a different course of action to be considered.

Next, consider the timing they assumed. If the timing were shorter or longer, would the trend change? For example, if it were longer, then competitors would have more time to react, or technology might change, or customer preferences might evolve. Make sure the assumptions on timing for implementation are not too optimistic. If needed, revise the numbers, and then reconsider potential courses of action.

Finally, spend some brain calories to design a quick experiment or test to get more certainty about key numbers. This could be a market test, a promotion, a limited process change, etc. Given the results of such experiments, you may want to revise the numbers and the potential courses of action.

Here is a good mindset: If you had to decide this issue a year from now, what information would you like to have gained? Can you get some of that now?

Judgment: Using the information and the opinions of advisors

First, remove passion and bias. Emotions don't help your reasoning, or your advisor's. A couple techniques are using value-neutral words, and evaluating problems not people. If you think a person is the problem, then think through why it is in their interests to behave the way they do. Then change those incentives. You won't change the person, but you can change their behavior, and that is the real issue.

Removing bias—both advisors' and yours—starts with seriously considering each step of the logic. What if the assumption at that step is wrong? Would that change the expected outcome? If it does, then dig into that step. Are they ignoring the risks because they've fallen in love with a particular approach? Do they have something to gain from that approach? Are they assuming that some prior experience will be repeated here, even if the situation is clearly different? Get another opinion!

Second, here are some techniques for assessing alternatives you created, or those suggested by advisors.

a. Does the recommended course solve the problem—does it meet the solution criteria?

b. "I heard your recommended approach. What is your second-best approach? What would have to happen for that to be better than your first recommendation?" Then you can assess a new scenario.

c. Re-anchor to your vision for the company. See Chapter 1 in *Business Techniques in Troubled Times*. Which course fits best with that vision?

d. Ask the advisor (or yourself) for all the reasons you should say no to his recommendation. These are the "cons." Evaluate whether they outweigh the pros.

e. Ask advisors "What is our response if your recommendation fails to achieve the solution criteria?" Is that scenario acceptable?

f. Were there people in the advisory group who disagreed with the group's recommendation? Talk to them and understand their thinking.

g. Anticipate several rounds of action and reaction by competitors and customers. This helps identify "unintended consequences," which could make that course of action unacceptable.

h. What if the timing changed? Maybe you could do it all at once, or in slower steps. Maybe the scenario assumes that all goes well and all dates are met, which hardly ever happens! Would different timing, usually slower, change the expected outcomes? Would it be safer, giving you more time to adjust if expectations turned out to be wrong?

Americans, especially men, tend to pride themselves on being decision-makers, which means deciding quickly. A fast decision that does not solve, or worsens, the problem is nothing to be proud of! It takes a bit more humility to recognize that you don't have all the information needed, and neither do your advisors. The best decisions can result if we take a little more time to set up the Framework, validate our assumptions, make sure we have several alternatives to assess, and then examine why our first reaction might be wrong.

The French have a saying that translates roughly as "I was in error but not at fault." If you decide without testing assumptions and alternatives, without anticipating consequences and competitor and customer reactions, you will be both in error *and* at fault!

9.4 Decision-Making: Ethics and Resistance Both Require Humble Leadership

We all want to live according to our values—the kind of behavior we believe is right and fair. This is ethical behavior. But just like employees who are seduced by bad incentives into performing below standard, decision-makers can be tempted to ignore their own values. The reasons range from greed to power to fear and beyond. These are powerful motivators, so we need simple and strong anchors to make sure our decisions consider the interests of all those affected.

"Listen at the Heart of the Spider Web"

First, make yourself aware of the impact of your decision. When considering which course of action to choose, make the effort to see and feel beyond your own motivations. Like a spider at the middle of the web, you must feel all the tensions, influences, and emotions. Ask yourself these questions:

- Who is affected? Consider employees, customers, shareowners, community, and lenders.

- How does this decision affect them?

- What will be their first reaction?

- Will you have to work hard to explain why you decided this way?

- How would you feel about this decision if you were one of these groups?

Second, evaluate your thinking in terms of its impact vs. your values.

- How would you explain your decision to your mother, who is often the source of your values?

- Assume a local newspaper is reporting on your decision, using its own "value words." Would you be embarrassed? Would your explanation be simple and convincing?

Third, use some imagination to tweak your decision to minimize negative effects on various groups.

- Have you been reasoning from a single value (e.g. short-term profit)? Consider other values like fairness and doing the least harm.

- Consider the idea of prudence. Could you modify your decision so it is less drastic, allows for your assumptions and projections being wrong, and minimizes harsh impacts?

- Can you modify the timing or scope of your decision to do less harm, without losing much of the benefits?

The best decisions are balanced. They achieve the solution criteria (goals) while doing the least harm. They also recognize that your reasoning and forecasts could be wrong, and provide escape routes when that turns out to be true, before too much damage occurs. No one can see the future with perfect accuracy. A little humility at decision time can save your business when events prove you wrong, as they always will!

Don't Be Surprised When Some Key People Resist Your Decision

You can expect some resistance when you describe your decision. If it was hard for you to decide, it will be just as hard for them to see why you decided that way. Your response to resistance can make things better or worse.

First, share the decision and the thinking behind it *privately* with those affected. If there are too many individuals, select one, or a few. Consider this a trial explanation, and be open to changing your decision. This is not a test of your authority or your courage—it's an appeal for advice. The private approach makes it easier to modify your plan before publicly committing to it.

Second, really hear their concerns. Resist the natural tendency to try to persuade them by aggressively defending your thinking. Instead, listen and question to find the source of their concerns. Together, understand why those concerns are a problem for them.

Third, find a low-risk and speedy way to test and measure the impact of their concerns. This shows you really heard them and respect their thinking. Then you will both learn whether these issues require changes in the plan.

Fourth, ask them to suggest how the plan could be changed to satisfy their concerns and still solve the problem. This shows respect, and makes them your partner. Think through their suggestions together, so you both agree on the wisdom of any changes. As a result, they will support the revised plan with others. You will have their buy-in rather than their resistance.

Dealing with resistance this way calls for humility. You are asking for help, and listening. You are not the "great and powerful Oz" with all the answers. Being the one who must decide does not mean you are the only thinker and have all the answers.

Behave like an orchestrator rather than a dictator to get the best decisions and the best buy-in.

Did you notice that humility is the leadership style that gets the best results for both Ethics and Resistance? Respect your people, and they will respect you. Then you can move forward together, and implementation will have a much better chance to succeed.

9.5 Checklist for Making Good Decisions

Making a good decision is a process. It happens over time, not in an instant. As you ponder your decision, consider this checklist of reminders for good decision-making.

1. Delegate

Let your people decide, if they are closer to the situation. Coach them and provide some limits, and then encourage them to decide for themselves. Their morale will improve, their decisions are likely to be as good as yours (with practice and feedback), and you can save your efforts for the major decisions.

2. Decide

Problems rarely solve themselves. As time goes on, events tend to decide for you, limiting your options more and more. You must find a balance between "paralysis by analysis" and snap decisions. Let's call that balance "prudence." It involves due consideration, and validating your usually-biased assumptions, but it also means being aware of the perils of delay. There are no rewards for being the fastest to decide (no "manhood points"), but you will not be happy if you wait so long that events decide for you.

3. Understand Timing

Throughout the decision process, time can be both a friend and an enemy. It's an enemy when you let it push you into a premature decision, or when you avoid making a decision until events have forced you into a corner, or when you decide to take a drastic action before preparing for the effects.

Time is your friend if you start the decision process early enough so you have time to consult advisors, listen to employee concerns, and test assumptions before making commitments. Time can also be your friend if you stretch it out after deciding: gather the resources and prepare the audience before implementing, and implement in stages, so you have opportunities to adjust. The idea of "ripeness" is useful here.

4. Use a Framework

A Framework organizes your thinking. Use it to define the problem, select the relevant facts and numbers, decide what a good solution must achieve, identify the key unknowns, and imagine at least three alternative courses of action. Then you can assess the alternatives, using advisors to offset your blind spots.

5. Work Hard at Defining the Problem

What you see is only a symptom. The real problem is what is causing those symptoms. Ask yourself "Why?" several times to get to the real problem. For example, you see a customer problem. It seems to result from employee behavior. Are there other potential causes? Why do the employees behave that way? What benefit do they gain from that? Can you rearrange their incentives?

Here's an old saying to guide you: "Let not your first thought be your last thought." Einstein captured the importance of defining the problem correctly when he said: "If I were given one hour to save the planet, I would spend 59 minutes defining the problem and one minute resolving it."[33]

6. Check Your Attitude at the Door

a. Attitude toward people

Solve the problem, not the person. Use value-neutral words when you describe the problem, background, solution criteria, and key questions. It's not you against them. It's you against the problem.

If the problem seems to be someone's behavior, keep asking, "Why they do that?" It's probably not because they *want* to be a problem! It's more likely they don't know the effect of their actions, and they get some benefit by acting that way. If you can change the underlying cause, the behavior will change. For example, change the incentives so they get no benefit from acting that way, and get some benefit from acting the way you prefer. You will not win a frontal attack on behavior in the long term, so work on the causes of that behavior.

b. Attitude toward the opinions of others

Again, it is not you against them; it is you against the problem. With a dose of humility, you will see that others know things you don't, and they see things through biases different than yours. They can help you recognize your own biases in the assumptions you are making. Others may assess risk differently than you.

Others can help you see unintended consequences, and implementation problems. Don't battle to have your idea win the day—battle to find the best idea. See yourself as the orchestrator, not the dictator.

c. Attitude toward consistency

Do not reason from a single principle—that would be neither prudent nor pragmatic. Take a wider view, considering how others are affected. Be willing to make exceptions to previous positions if the conditions or situation have changed. You might even have been wrong before! If so, the sooner you realize it, the better. Keep an open mind.

7. Test and Quantify Your Assumptions

You will never have all the information you need before deciding, so you make assumptions. Two cautions can guide you here.

- First, quantify the impact of not just your facts but your assumptions as well. You may assume something and evaluate it as bad, but that does not mean it is important. You won't know that until you quantify it and/or its effect. You can quantify by doing more research into your own company's experience, seeking other company experience, or creating a quick test in the real world. Don't rely on possibly flawed logic and assumptions about the market. Instead, experiment. For example, try it with a few customers or for part of a week, and see what happens.

- Second, recognize that bias can play a major role in your assumptions. This is why you test them, and why you get the advice of others (but you must recognize their biases as well).

You will need numbers to decide, so quantify everything you can. Your Framework's Background Section (relevant facts) should be filled with numbers as well as words.

8. Create Multiple Alternative Courses of Action, and Then Assess Them

Create at least three courses of action, forcing yourself to open up to other possibilities beyond your first reaction. The worst decisions are those framed as go/no go for one course of action. The best decisions use different perspectives to create different approaches, so you can consider many angles, and perhaps blend some of them into a well-rounded decision. Remember, "let not your first thought be your last thought."

When you create your alternatives, you will make a quick list of pros and cons for each. Then you evaluate these pros and cons. How good are the pros? How bad are the cons? How much will they cost? Having the alternatives tells you what to investigate, so establish them first and then assess them.

This is the time to ask for the views of others, after you've organized the situation into a Framework and developed some alternatives. Their views can change the whole framework, from problem statement to which facts are relevant to imagining new alternatives. Be humble, ask why, and listen to learn. The goal is not to persuade them; it's to gain insight so you can make a better decision.

9. Ethics: "Listen at the Heart of the Spider Web"

This phrase is about feeling the impact of your decision on all those it affects. How would you feel if that were you? What can you do to minimize negative effects and still achieve most of your goal? Perhaps some more imaginative timing, or carving out some exceptions, would ease the pain.

10. Work Hard at "Unintended Consequences"

Decisions made for good reasons can turn out to be bad if they cause others to react in unforeseen ways. We see examples every day in the political realm. Intentions are good, but foresight is bad. Defense against this risk starts with humility. You could be wrong! Customers, competitors, or employees could do something other than what you predict! Maybe you don't understand their needs or their choices as well as you thought.

Working hard at "unintended consequences" means imagining several rounds of reaction to your decision, and assuming it is misunderstood at the outset. Test your imaginings with some members of these groups. Then adapt your decision to minimize the unexpected behaviors.

11. Implementation Requires Forethought; It's Not an Afterthought

Paraphrasing Edison, solutions are 10% inspiration (the decision), and 90% perspiration (implementation). Think through implementation resources and timing *before* you finally decide, because inability to get it done when planned could drive you to choose a different course of action. The timing or stages of implementation can be the difference between a drastic solution and a balanced one. Recognize that implementation always happens later than planned, at greater cost, with less effectiveness. After all, we're human! Given that, is it still a good idea?

Selling Your
Small Business

Selling Your Small Business

THE ULTIMATE PAYOFF FOR GROWING YOUR BUSINESS is the opportunity to sell it to fund either retirement or your next venture. Growing businesses attract buyers. Without growth, buyers are harder to find and unwilling to pay a good price. Unfortunately, the skills you developed to manage and grow the business do not prepare you to sell it. This last section of the book explains the business sales process so you can prepare for yourself and the business to win the payoff for your life's work.

Part Five Driving Concepts

- Selling your business is the end result of a thoughtful process, beginning when you started or bought into the business. It takes time. You must assess your business and its value drivers like a buyer would, "fix" any issues that would concern the buyer, and protect and improve those value drivers in the months and years leading up to the sale.

- The biggest value drivers for a small business are whether the owner's personal involvement is crucial to success, and the concentration of revenue, i.e., what percentage of company revenue comes from the top one, two, five, and ten customers.

- Valuation considers the past three years' financial results, growth prospects, industry risk, and company risk, as well as the transaction prices for similar size companies in the same industry. The most common basis for valuation is a multiple of EBITDA (earnings before interest, tax, depreciation, and amortization). EBITDA is basically operating margin plus depreciation. The multiple could be two to five times for most small businesses. The valuation is expressed as a range.

- A business broker will write the Offering Memorandum, use their contacts to find buyers, qualify them, and suggest negotiating positions for the owner. The broker may also recommend a deal attorney and accountant. Brokers charge around 10% of the selling price.

- Buyers often want to delay paying for the business to get the seller's help in the transition, and to hold the seller accountable for their statement of the business situation and prospects. Techniques include seller financing, earn-out, and escrow for representations and warranties.

- Due diligence by the buyer begins when the seller believes they can make a deal. Sellers are wise to begin early to gather all the documents buyers want to see. The real deal term negotiations happen after due diligence. Once a deal is signed, there is usually a time interval before it closes. Perhaps 90 days are needed to accomplish "closing conditions," such as agreement and approval by other parties and regulators.

Techniques Presented in Part Five

Topic	Technique	Content	Articles
Selling Your Business: Overview and Preparation	Overview	Describes five stages of the selling process, including role of business broker.	10.1
	Valuation	Two valuation methods: comparables and discounted cash flow. Identifies discounts for industry and company.	10.2
	Major Changes before Sale	Change the business prior to sale to avoid discounts to its value and to maximize selling price.	10.3
	Minor Changes before Sale	Tidy management attracts more buyers and better prices.	10.4
	Owner Goals	Consider alternatives to sale, modified timing of sale, and different deal structures to suit owner goals.	10.5
	Documents Needed	Lists 29 documents needed for the sale process.	10.6
	Identifying Buyers	Strategic buyers pay more. Finding buyers yourself can reduce fees to business broker.	11.1
	Qualifying Buyers	Process for exchanging information with buyers to sort out those who are serious.	11.2
	Negotiating Deal Terms	Lists basic deal terms and additional deal terms often proposed by buyers.	12.1
	Seller Financing	Defines seller financing and its risks. Suggests techniques to reduce those risks.	12.2

	Earn-out	Defines the earn-out concept, lists benefits and risks, and the types of terms to be negotiated.	12.3
Selling Your Business: Overview and Preparation	Representations, Warranties, and Escrow	Defines how these terms operate and why they are used. Provides statistics.	12.4
	How Advisors Add Value	Wording issues for disclosures and indemnity.	12.5
	Due Diligence Overview	Explains the due diligence process. Recommends the seller's attitude and preparation.	13.1
	Due Diligence Checklist	Lists dozens of types of documents which may be sought by buyers, in five categories.	13.2
	Due Diligence and Deal Terms	Explains what the buyer does with due diligence findings. Techniques involve reps and warranties, asset sales, and exclusion of selected assets or liabilities.	13.3
	Closing Conditions	Lists various closing conditions and deliverables. Techniques include "bring-down" of reps and warranties, and working capital adjustment.	13.4

Chapter 10: Overview and Preparing for Sale

10.1 Overview: Selling Your Business

Will you be able to sell your small business? The answer depends on whether a buyer can envision operating it without your own personal role in customer relationships and delivering the product or service. The less it depends on you, the more likely it can be sold.

Selling your business is the end result of a thoughtful process, beginning when you started or bought into the business. It takes time. You must assess your business and its value drivers like a buyer would, "fix" any issues that would concern a buyer, and protect and improve those value drivers in the months and years leading up to the sale.

When is a good *time to sell*? The best time is when you don't need to—when the business is growing, results are good, and no personal or other deadline could force you to settle for less than the best offer. Buyers are looking for a business with three consecutive years of growing revenue and profits.

The best time *to decide* to sell your business is two to three years before you expect the sale to be completed. This gives you

- one to two years to get the business ready for sale, and

- one to two years for the sales process itself.

Getting the business ready for sale has major and minor components. The major ones involve minimizing the effect of valuation "discounts" that could make your business worth less. Examples are dependence on only a few customers, and dependence on the owner's unique role in sustaining business operations. Minor get-ready activities include improving the website, documenting processes and governance, and improving the appearance of the facilities. Articles 10.3 and 10.4 address "getting the business ready for sale."

The Sales Process itself may take six to nine months if the first deal does not fall through, or longer if it does. The process has five stages: preparation; solicit and qualify buyers; negotiating the offer; due diligence; and closing.

Should You Use a Business Broker?

Business brokers offer to be your guide and act as your middle-man/spokesperson with the buyer or his broker. They handle the sales process while you manage the business. The result is a higher selling price and a faster sales process compared to doing it yourself. Brokers will advise you on getting the business ready for sale, develop the Offering Memorandum including a valuation of the business, distribute it to their own network and various websites to attract buyers, qualify and assess potential buyers, and negotiate with the buyers on your behalf.

Brokers charge approximately 10% to 12% of the purchase price, with a minimum payment of $7000 to $9000. You may negotiate for fewer functions and a lower fee, if you believe you can perform some of these functions yourself or find a consultant to do them for less.

Stage One: Preparation

The sales process depends on an Offering Memorandum (OM). This document describes the business: its product, market, competition, operations, performance for the last three years, and financial situation. Typical length may be 12 to 20 pages. This Memorandum will include a selling price for the business, which means a valuation of the business (see next article) must have been done before the Memorandum is complete. The OM presents the business honestly and attractively.

After getting the business ready for sale and performing the valuation to find an asking price, the next step is gathering data to write the Offering Memorandum. As part of this process, you assess the business strengths and weaknesses, opportunities and threats (SWOT). These factors affect the valuation.

Before sending the Offering Memorandum to any potential buyer, you develop other short documents.

- The Teaser is a one-page summary of the business, its highlights, the asking price, and who to contact. It cites the industry and operating area, but may not name the business.

- A summary of the Offering Memorandum may be used, to provide more information than the Teaser while excluding key customer and financial data. Its purpose is to keep buyers interested as you ask them to provide information showing they are qualified to buy.

- The Non-Disclosure Agreement (NDA) is a contract stating that the person asking for the full Offering Memorandum will not disclose its information or use it in his own business.

- The buyer qualification questionnaire is a set of questions that enable you to reject buyers that do not appear to be seriously interested in or capable of buying the business.

Finally, you will need to create the "Corporate Book," containing the OM and some of the key documents backing up its assertions.

Stage 2: Solicit and Qualify Buyers

To solicit buyers, you or your agent/broker distributes the Teaser, promising to send the summary (if used) and the full Offering Memorandum to those who are interested. Responders must sign the NDA and submit answers to the buyer qualification questionnaire. Those who do, and who are accepted, receive the Memorandum. The broker's network of contacts and websites can be useful in this stage, though you may choose to solicit your own set of contacts first. If a few potential buyers emerge from your own list, you may pay a lower fee to the broker.

While this solicitation process is running its course, you should be gathering documents for the buyer to review in Due Diligence (Stage 4). You'll also make a list of information about the buyer that you wish to review during the Due Diligence stage.

Stage 3: Negotiating the Offer

A buyer's request to negotiate (Expression of Interest) triggers Stage 3. You should obtain guidance for this stage, using an experienced deal lawyer or a broker or both. Interested potential buyers usually request a meeting to discuss the material provided, some of their due diligence concerns, and some potential deal terms. After the meeting, they will submit a non-binding Letter of Intent (LOI), with a price and deal terms contingent on full due diligence findings. After Due Diligence, serious negotiations on deal terms take place.

Although deal term negotiations happen both before and after Due Diligence, we discuss deal terms first because the seller may reject the LOI based on preliminary discussions, and refuse to allow further due diligence.

The buyer who sends a letter of intent committing to a price and offering earnest money (deposit) may also request exclusive rights to negotiate on the sale for a certain time period. Do not grant exclusivity to anyone who does not offer earnest money and a committed price in writing.

The offered price is a beginning point for negotiations. Usually the points negotiated fall into three categories: price, terms, and deal structure. "Terms" can include concerns like environmental assurances, transition assistance, staffing plans, or assumption of existing obligations. "Deal structure" means purchase of only assets vs. the entire business; the amount paid; timing and form of payment (e.g. cash or stock or goods); and any contingencies that could affect the amount or timing.

After the two parties agree to general parameters on the price, terms, and deal structure, each of them provides a "disclosure statement" to the other. This is a list of pertinent facts about the business and the buyer, which the party guarantees are true. There will be some negotiations over these disclosure statements, with the buyer demanding stronger assurances of business health and growth prospects than the seller is willing to guarantee.

Stage 4: Due Diligence

In Stage 4 each party examines documents provided by the other party to validate "Disclosure Statement" assurances. This examination is called "Due Diligence." The process may also include interviews with employees, unions, accountants, suppliers, or even key customers. It may involve site visits or other ways to gather information. When the two parties are finished, they either accept the Disclosure Statements as given or agree on revisions. Then they finalize price and deal terms, and then sign a Purchase Agreement. This completes the "signing" of the deal, but does not complete the transaction. The documents signed will contain Closing Conditions, as noted below.

Stage 5: Closing

Usually the two parties agree on some actions that must be taken before the transaction is actually completec. These are called "Closing Conditions." Examples include regulatory or lender approvals, obtaining financing, some transition assistance by the seller, provision of certain missing documents, and assignment of leases. Once the Closing Conditions are satisfied, which may take 30 to 90 days, the two parties sign a Purchase Agreement that includes the entire deal and notes the completion of the Closing Conditions.

10.2 Valuation and Discounts: Setting a Price for Your Business

How much is your business worth? It's worth whatever a buyer will pay. As a rule of thumb, this might be two to five times last year's operating margin, if it includes your salary as an expense.

A successful sales process results in agreement by buyer and seller on the value of the business. The first step toward this agreement is the seller's estimate of the value of the business ("valuation"), which leads to the "asking price."

Valuation estimates the value of a business to a buyer (not to the seller) using two methods: "comparable" transaction prices, and expected future cash flows. The issue is not value to the current owner. Valuation is about "transferable value," i.e., value to the buyer. Future cash flows are forecasted considering "normalized earnings" for the past three years, and growth projections. Then the future cash flow forecast is *discounted* to account for the risk that the business results may fall short of expectations.

"Normalized earnings" modifies financial results to show a fair salary for the owner and to remove expenses that are not critical to business success once it is transferred to a new owner.

What Is Cash Flow?

Cash flow is defined as EBITDA: Earnings Before Interest, Taxes, Depreciation, and Amortization. Usually EBITDA is calculated as Operating Margin plus (or before) Depreciation, since depreciation is a booked expense that does not actually affect cash flow. Practically-speaking, cash flow is the money available to the business owner to pay interest and taxes, and then use the remainder to reinvest in the business, pay debt principal, or distribute as profits.

In a small business, EBITDA might be understated because expenses are overstated. This can happen when the owner increases expenses more than necessary to reduce profits to minimize taxes. The extra expense items are usually dual-use items that benefit the owner personally as well as the business. Some examples are owner salary to the extent it exceeds market norms, health and other insurance, gym and club memberships, subscriptions, vehicle costs, and maybe some office expenses.

When it comes time to sell, the owner wants the buyer to consider those dual-use expenses as part of cash flow and not as expenses, that is, to see them as part of EBITDA. The name for such a revised EBITDA is Seller Discretionary Benefits or Earnings. Some buyers may not accept this type of adjustment, so it makes sense for buyers to limit such "discretionary" expenses in the year before sale, lest a lower EBITDA result in a lower selling price.

Method 1: "Comparable" Transactions

"Comparable" transactions are the purchase prices of similar size companies in the seller's industry or similar industries. The analyst is looking for similarities in revenues, number of employees, product or service line, geography served, etc. This is the same kind of process used to appraise a house by looking at the selling prices of similar houses sold in the same neighborhood in the past few months.

Your company's North American Industrial Classification (NAIC) code is the starting point to look at the right industries for comparable transactions, so be sure to include the right NAIC code in your Offering Memorandum. Find NAIC codes on-line or in databases at your library.

The comparable companies are not identical to yours, so their selling prices are not directly used for comparison. Instead, the valuation analyst calculates each firm's selling price as a multiple of its last year's EBITDA and revenue.

A high multiple means that buyers feel the business has excellent growth potential and low strategic risk, such as risk that the product will become a commodity, or that the business will be bypassed by a new technology. A low multiple means the opposite: low growth and/or high risk. For example, wireless phone companies may sell at a multiple of 9 or 10 due to growth, but wireline phone companies attract multiples of only 5 to 6, due to their risk of being unprofitable as their subscribers shift to wireless and cable.

Small businesses normally sell at a multiple around two to five times EBITDA, with most being sold at the lower end of the range. If their EBITDA is 33% of revenue, 3 x EBITDA is the same as 1 x Revenue.

Method 2: Forecasting Cash Flow

The valuation analyst does a "discounted cash flow" (DCF) forecast for the business. This process creates an income statement for each of the next three to five years using revenue, expenses, and growth rates provided by the seller. The analyst calculates the resulting cash flow, and discounts the outcomes for risks and expected inflation. The result is the *present value* of these future cash flows after reducing them for risks.

Applying Discounts to the Forecasted Cash Flow

The higher the discount rate, the lower the present value of the business will be. Some risk factors considered in determining discount rates are:

- Risk-free rate of return (T-Bills): buyer could earn this much without risk, and he is taking risk buying this business, so the business cash flows are discounted by this amount (around 3%).

- Equity risk: the risk of owning stock, rather than making a loan where collateral could be claimed if forecasts prove too optimistic (around 7%).

- Small company risk: recognizes the greater risk in small companies due lack of resources when a downturn occurs (around 6%).

- Industry risk: varies by type of industry (around 2%).

The above discounts are general or industry-based. They total to 18%. Other discounts may also apply for the company's own unique situation, such as:

* Owner's role is critical to success: the risk is that the buyer cannot maintain the owner's relationships, or replace his role in operations, without additional cost.

* Concentration of customers: if one customer accounts for more than 10% of revenue, discount rises because business viability is at risk if that customer were to leave.

* Stable employees and management: risk increases if high employee turnover is expected, so the business is worth less.

* Company historical results and growth trends.

* Growth trends in the region where the company operates.

I've seen these company discounts total to 27%, or 44% when added to the industry discounts above. To avoid such high discounts, owners may wish to change the business before selling, thereby getting a better sales price. See Article 10.3.

The Valuation Is a Range

The analyst's final step is to assemble the findings. One to three comparable ranges may be provided, such as a multiple of EBITDA, multiple of Revenue, and/or multiple of some other industry indicator (such as lines in the phone business, or square feet in retail).

The range of value for each of these measures will be the lowest comparable transaction's measure (e.g. 1.6 x EBITDA) to the highest (e.g. 3.5 x EBITDA), after excluding exceptional cases.

You end up with three ranges, each with a midpoint indicated. The average or median of the three midpoints is the value of the business based on comparable transactions. This is what buyers have actually paid for similar businesses in recent years.

The fourth range will be based on the DCF analysis plus and minus 20%–30%, so that the actual DCF analysis outcome is the midpoint of this fourth range.

At this point, valuation is complete. Then you pick your asking price, knowing that the buyer will be doing the same valuation process.

10.3 Getting Your Business Ready for Sale— Major Changes

The time a small business owner spends getting the business ready for sale may be the most profitable hours of his entire career! Improvements made pre-sale can result in a significant increase in selling price.

What to Change: Understand Target Buyers

To sell any product, the first step is to understand the target market. This is true for selling a business as well as selling a product. The owner and his advisors identify types of buyers who could make more of the business than the owner could. Maybe they have more resources, or complementary businesses, or could cut overhead because they are already in the business.

Two general buyer categories are financial vs. strategic. Financial buyers are simply buying a cash flow, without being able to take advantage of other economies or growth opportunities. Strategic buyers are already in the business, or a related one, so they may be able to earn greater returns (and hence pay more to buy the business) by combining their existing operations with the acquired business. These are called "synergies." Examples include consolidating operations, or selling a broader product line through existing channels, either to their existing customers or to your current customers.

Understanding the target market of buyers tells the owner what to change to become more attractive to those buyers. For example, if they are already in the business, you don't want to invest in a new machine or new building they may already have.

What to Change: Understand the Value Drivers of the Business

"Value Drivers" are the business characteristics that either reduce the new owner's risk or enhance growth opportunities. Here's a "top ten" list of value drivers, based on *Master Ten Value Drivers to Sell Your Business at the Highest Price* by Rose Stabler:[34]

1. Stable and predictable cash flow

2. Reliable financial information

3. Human capital/quality of workforce

4. Customer diversity

5. Growth potential

6. Operating systems and procedures

7. Facility and equipment condition

8. Goodwill/relationships

9. Barriers to competitive entry

10. Product diversity

The best way to maximize the selling price of a business is to manage these ten value drivers. The better they are, the more buyers will be interested, and the more they will pay.

Major Changes to Get Ready for Sale

As noted in the previous article, the discounting considerations in the valuation process can reduce the selling price significantly. Discounts to value reflect the risk to the buyer from weaknesses in these ten value drivers, so it makes sense to change the business in order to reduce or avoid such discounts. For a small business, the most important are items 3 and 4 in the above list: the role of the owner in operations and sales, and concentration of customers.

A sale-ready business can run without the seller's involvement. This may be inconceivable to a small business owner-operator who has spent a lifetime of effort and anguish to build his or her business. Nevertheless, the pool of potential buyers is much larger if they do not need to have the skill, experience, and energy to conduct operations as well as manage the business itself.

To get ready for sale, the owner must replace his own role in operations and sales. The first step is usually operations. Promote or hire someone to do the operations work the owner had been doing. Take the time to train the new person. Compensate them well if they agree (in writing) to stay at least two years under new owners.

The second step is sales. Decide if your new operations manager can also fulfill your sales role. If not, hire someone to replace you in sales. Again, take the time to train your sales replacement in customer relationships, developing bids or quotes, and the judgment involved in negotiations and customer service. As above, compensate them well if they agree to stay two years under new owners.

After taking three to six months to find and train these "replacements," the owner has extra time, perhaps three or four days per week! Rather than micro-manage your replacements, use this time to work on the second major change—finding new customers.

To reduce risk for buyers, and to reduce discounting the value of your business, you want to find enough customers so that no one customer accounts for more than 10% of revenue, and you serve customers in at least two industries with different cycles or success drivers. This reduces risk in the event that one industry experiences a downturn.

Finding new customers and opening new markets takes time and effort. That time was not available while the owner was involved in operations, but it *will* be available once the owner has replaced his operations and sales roles. This effort can take two years to bear fruit and show up in your financials. *This is why you decide to sell as long as two years before the sale process itself starts!*

10.4 Getting Your Business Ready for Sale— Minor Changes

We learned in high school that an attractive first impression makes other people interested in knowing more about us. The same is true when selling your business.

Buyers are attracted to businesses that appear to be well-managed. They prefer to avoid surprises after the transaction. Seeing tidy management before the deal gives them confidence that the business will run well after they buy it. The pay-off for tidy management is more buyers and a higher selling price for the business.

Website

The website is the business' front door. A well-designed website implies a well-designed business. Revamping your website may take several months, and you should complete it before beginning the sales process.

Organize your website by customer group. Hopefully you are serving more than one industry or segment, to reduce risk of customer concentration. The home page should have an entry point for each of these customer groups. Then the pages for each group should be organized around their needs. Your products or services make sense only in relation to customer needs.

Your site will have plenty of content, attractive and uncrowded graphics, and error-free navigation and spelling. The content shows how your services are different from competitor offerings. It also emphasizes the benefits customers gain from those differences (your "positioning"). Your service offerings are grouped into three tiers, with names communicating basic, standard, and premium. Customers can order a tier plus additional *a la carte* services.

Be sure to include success stories and testimonials to prove credibility. See Article 10.3 in *Business Techniques in Troubled Times*.

Marketing Materials

Your marketing materials invite customers to your front door, the website. They must be up-to-date and consistent with the website's message and appearance. They convey your positioning with a clear message and graphics. Test a variety of marketing materials for each of your customer segments to find which get the best results.

Appearance of the Facility and Equipment

First impressions matter. Just as sellers of houses invest in the appearance of their house before putting it up for sale (called "staging"), business owners can get the best selling price when their place of business appears well-organized, clean, and has books and records readily-available. Remove clutter, clean and spruce up the premises, and organize your records!

Operations Documentation

Most small businesses do not take the time to document how they operate, but do so if you want to demonstrate topnotch management to a buyer. The impression is:

"This business is well-organized. They know how they do things, and they do things in a consistent way. They have anticipated problems and limited their impact, so I can be confident even about the things I don't know."

In this way, documentation makes the sales process faster and keeps buyers interested. Here are some examples of operational documentation:

- Process maps for key processes, with standards of acceptable performance

- Standardization in bills of materials, quotes, and wherever else possible

- Quality control standards and quality measurement process

- Job descriptions

- Training and job aids, i.e., small reminders of how to do a task, posted near the work station

- Employee manual

- Organization chart

- Delegated limits of authority

- Floor and circuit layouts, and emergency (fire) procedures

Governance Documentation

"Governance" has to do with the way decisions are made and the business is administered. Documentation of governance means the written policies that define who does what, who makes what decisions, and even what they consider when they make those decisions. These are often called "company policies."

Governance documentation also includes evidence that certain decisions actually were made, such as minutes of the board of directors, annual reports, regulatory filings, tax filings, and announcements to employees. In addition to signifying good management, having these documents can also prevent unpleasant legal consequences.

Documents for Due Diligence

Many of the documents required for the buyer's review during Due Diligence should be gathered during the preparation stage, because they are needed to prepare the Offering Memorandum. Examples are three years of the business tax returns and three years of the business income statements and balance sheets. Article 10.6 provides a list of all the documents needed for Due Diligence.

Assembling these documents into binders sorted by subject matter makes the buyer's Due Diligence effort go smoothly. This is more evidence of good management, making the business more attractive to buyers.

Valuation of Intellectual Property

Owners have the alternative of selling or licensing their intellectual property (IP), rather than selling the business. This may make sense if the IP seems to have more value than the business at the time of sale. If so, calculating the value of the IP is worth doing before trying to sell the business. Methods for valuation of IP are not as settled as they are for hard assets or for entire businesses, but there are firms who perform this service.

All these activities can result in a higher selling price, but they take time to implement—perhaps six to nine months if they are not all undertaken at the same time.

10.5 Owner Goals and Selling the Business

Before selling the business, owners should take a moment to consider their goals at this moment. There may be other ways to meet the goals. There may also be interim steps, so that timing becomes a tool to maximize returns.

The Goals in this table are about time and effort. The strategy alternatives consider different selling approaches, tailored to the adjacent goal.

- **Time:** Do you need all the proceeds of a sale now, or a large portion of them, or are you simply establishing a retirement fund to be drawn on over decades?

- **Effort:** Do you really need to sell now, or is your real goal just to find a way to cut back your own day-to-day involvement?

Owner Goal	Strategy Alternatives
1. Capture the value of the business to create a retirement fund for the owner, to be drawn on monthly over decades.	A. Sell business to employees gradually via ESOP; reap tax advantages. B. Sell the business and reinvest after-tax proceeds. Accept payment terms that maximize price, e.g. earn-out; stock swap or stock payment; owner-financing.
2. Capture the value of the business to pay for a large immediate expense.	C. Sell the business and reinvest after-tax proceeds. May accept earn-out or partial payment in stock.
3. Work less—reduce the time and effort the owner devotes to the business.	D. Hire managers to perform owner's operational functions; owner works 1-2 days/week on getting new customers; retain profits now and sell in 2-3 years. — May sell only a portion of the business, retaining some stake
4. Exit now, before a change in the business environment reduces its value.	E. Sell the business and reinvest after-tax proceeds. No "earn-out." Cash payment, not stock.

Key Point

The longer you can wait for the deal to mature and pay out, the more likely you will capture the highest selling price and the best tax treatment for proceeds.

However, waiting involves risk. Changing conditions may diminish the buyer's ability to make deferred payments as agreed.

Examples

If you can wait,

- You have time to change the business to improve valuation, per prior articles.
  - Risk: business results may weaken during change period.

- You can accept part of the selling price over two to four years after the sale based on business profits in those years, called an "earn-out." If the owner accepts this risk, the buyer needs less cash so he may be willing to pay more, and more buyers may find the deal feasible.
  - Risk: business results may fall short of target during earn-out period.

- You can accept part of the payment in the buyer's stock, and sell it in portions when it has a favorable market price, keeping your tax bracket low. Since the buyer will need less cash at the time of the closing, he may accept a higher selling price.
  - Risk: buyer's stock may lose value for any number of reasons.

- You can offer seller-financing to the buyer, being paid part of the selling price over five to ten years with interest.

Collateral is the business itself. Again, since the buyer would need less cash, the selling price may be higher.

- o Risk: buyer may be unable to pay the loan for any number of reasons; owner may not want to take over the business again; business value (collateral) may have declined to be less than the value of the loan between the sale and the time the former owner decides to call the loan and take over the business again.

- You can sell to employees at an appraised market valuation via an Employee Stock Ownership Plan (ESOP), getting the most favorable tax treatment for proceeds. See Chapter 16 in *Business Techniques in Troubled Times*.
  - o Risk: cost of administration.

Recommendation
Understand your own goals. Fit your strategy to them. Use time to enhance the value of the company. My preferred approach is to hire to replace one's owner/operator role, work one or two days per week on new customers, sell two to three years later, accept an earn-out or stock swap but not seller-financing, and use an ESOP if it appears feasible.

10.6 Documents Needed to Sell Your Business

The business is not what *you* say it is. It's what *the documents* say it is.

Business buyers want to minimize risk. They want to see the documents that prove the seller's assertions. You will need to gather the following documents, and organize them into binders to facilitate review by the buyer during the due diligence process.

Some of these documents will be needed to prepare the Offering Memorandum in Stage One. These documents go into the "Corporate Book." The remainder should be gathered and filed into binders during Stage Two, while you are waiting to receive offers. However, some of these other documents may also be filed in the "Corporate Book" provided to serious buyers prior to the Due Diligence stage. Such documents are marked with * in the list below.

Needed in Stage One

1. Financial Statements for current and past three years: balance sheet, income statement, tax return for business

2. Statement of Seller's Discretionary Earnings or cash flow

3. Financial ratios and trends

4. Photos of business

5. List of opportunities for improvement with revenue/profit projections for each

6. Marketing Plan and samples of marketing materials

7. Evidence of major obligations (loans, leases), customer commitments, and policy decisions.

Needed for Buyer's Due Diligence

8. Governance documents: board minutes, policies, announcements to employees*

9. Note for seller financing

10. Accounts payable and accounts receivable aging reports

11. Inventory list with value detail

12. List of furnishings, fixtures, and equipment with value detail*

13. Asset depreciation schedule for tax returns

14. Supplier and distributor contracts*

15. Client list and major client contracts*

16. Staffing list with hire dates and salaries; employment contracts and Independent Contractor agreements*

17. Organization chart*

18. Business formation documents*

19. Leases*

20. Business licenses, certifications, and registrations*

21. Professional certificates

22. Insurance policies

23. Copies proving ownership of patents, trademarks, and other IP*

24. Outstanding loan agreements*

25. Description of liens*

26. Product or service descriptions and price lists*

27. Employment policy manual

28. Business procedures manual

29. Other documents unique to your business

Chapter 11: Identifying Buyers

11.1 Identifying Buyers for Your Business

Be ready before you try to sell the business! When you are ready to start the search for buyers, this is the situation:

- You know your goals, and the type of transaction that fits them best.

- You have optimized the business, making key changes to get it ready for sale.

- You have probably engaged a business broker.

- You have a valuation, and have identified a range of expectations for selling price, and decided what price to ask for.

- You have developed an Offering Memorandum, Teaser, and possibly a summary of the OM.

- You have also prepared several documents to use with buyers: a Confidentiality or Nondisclosure Agreement that covers both your information and whatever they disclose to you; a buyer profile questionnaire; and a buyer's personal financial statement template.

- You have developed a Corporate Book, and will create due diligence binders during the buyer search, adapting them later to address particular concerns expressed by potential buyers during preliminary discussions.

- You know what you want to see in a buyer's Expression of Interest or Letter of Intent.

First, Identify Potential Strategic Buyers

Typically, strategic buyers are operating in your industry, so they could achieve growth or efficiency synergies by acquiring your company. As a result, they will often be willing to pay a higher price than financial buyers. Since they are likely to offer the best price, it makes sense to solicit them first.

The business owner is the one most likely to know which companies or individuals might be strategic buyers. Consider your competitors, suppliers, and customers. Consider also companies who sell similar products in different markets than yours. If you were expanding your business, which of these would you be interested in buying? These may be the best candidates to buy your business.

However, approaching them may disclose the identity of your business, and this might hurt its performance or competitive position. When selling a business, one of the trade-offs is that attracting the widest market of buyers implies the greatest loss of confidentiality.

Techniques to minimize this risk include (1) masking the identity of the business until buyers appear to be both interested and qualified, (2) confidentiality agreement, and (3) using a broker to handle the communications rather than doing so yourself.

Second, Consider Your Own Network

Aside from people or companies you know that may be potential strategic buyers, your network will include people who may be financial buyers. Most importantly, your contacts may be able to forward your invitation to potential buyers in *their* networks. People are more likely to respond to an email from someone they know than to a broadcast from a broker.

Your network of connections may include:

- Some people in your email address book.

- Your LinkedIn connections.

- Members of LinkedIn groups such as industry-oriented groups or alumni from companies where you've worked.

- Members of associations you have joined, such as a Chamber of Commerce or a trade association.

You may invite them to forward your Teaser Announcement to people in their own networks, widening the circle even further.

Note that your deal with a business broker could provide for a reduced fee if the buyer turns out to be someone you identified, rather than someone responding to the broker's solicitations.

Third Priority: Business Broker Solicitations

In addition to serving as the middleman to deal with your contacts, one of the primary services of your business broker is their ability to reach a wider circle of potential buyers. Brokers use these channels of communication:

- Their own network of transaction professionals, who in turn have their own networks of potential buyers. These professionals include accountants, attorneys, bankers, and other brokers.

- Their own database of qualified potential buyers.

- Their own website and monthly newsletter.

- Memberships in subscription-based deal groups and websites.

- Brokers may also advertise on the web or at industry events, or even use direct mail.

11.2 Qualifying Buyers and Exchange of Information

Tired of "tirekickers"? Many of those who respond to the Teaser Announcement will not turn out to be serious buyers. They may be merely fishing for information. They may lack the necessary funds or industry qualifications. Brokers say this group can amount to 90% of responders. In the used car industry, they're called "tirekickers."

To avoid spending time on this type of responder, the seller uses a *qualifying* process and often assigns the broker to manage it. Thus the term "Seller" in the following process description also includes the broker acting as the seller's agent, if desired.

The Buyer Qualification Process

1. Seller sends Teaser Announcement.

2. Buyer sends Confidentiality Agreement, Buyer Profile, and Buyer's Personal Financial Statement.

3. Seller assesses Buyer according to Seller's requirements
   - Ability to pay cash required on closing date
   - Ability to finance purchase price (if Seller loan, what Buyer collateral is available?)
   - Buyer's timeframe vs. Seller's
   - Buyer's industry qualifications or other ability to operate the business.

4. If satisfied, Seller calls Buyer to discuss the transaction and seller's requirements in general terms.

5. Optional: If the Seller is satisfied and Buyer remains interested, Seller signs Confidentiality Agreement and sends OM summary without key information (customers, financials), and requests Proof of Funds from Buyer.

6. Optional: Buyer sends Proof of Funds.

7. If satisfied, Seller signs Confidentiality Agreement and sends OM, and requests the Buyer respond with a nonbinding Expression of Intent. Seller states what it should include, such as:
   - Buyer's expectation for type of transaction: purchase of assets or total business, cash, stock swap, cash plus earn-out, other
   - Buyer's price range, payment timing, and method of financing
   - Buyer's timeframe for closing
   - Buyer's qualifications to operate the business

– Buyer's need for transition assistance from Seller post-closing: expected duration, hours, and compensation.

8. If satisfied, Seller schedules a meeting with the Buyer.

Comments on the Process

When the buyer provides qualifying information, the seller provides more information about the business.

The process is a disciplined step-by-step procedure where buyers can be progressively qualified, protecting the seller from divulging information to parties who lack either legitimate interest or the financial resources to complete the transaction.

Recognizing that excessive confidentiality narrows the pool of buyers, sellers may decide to accept some confidentiality risk and combine some steps, such as excluding 5 and 6 above if they already know the financial strength of the buyer from Step 2. Once the process is complete, the Seller sends the Corporate Book to the buyer, and preliminary discussions on price and terms can begin.

Interested potential buyers usually request a meeting to discuss the material provided, some of their due diligence concerns, and some potential deal terms. After the meeting, they will submit a non-binding Letter of Intent (LOI), with a price and deal terms contingent on full due diligence findings. After Due Diligence (Stage 4), serious negotiations on deal terms take place.

Although deal term negotiations happen both before and after Due Diligence, we discuss deal terms first, in the next few articles, because the seller may reject the LOI based on preliminary discussions, and refuse to allow due diligence.

Chapter 12: Understanding Deal Terms

12.1 Negotiating Deal Terms for Selling Your Small Business

Every deal is a package deal. When you sell to your customers, your offer is a package of *deal terms*: what they are buying, how much they pay, when the money is due, shipping, return policy, etc. You know that if you change some of these deal terms, the price might change as well. The same idea applies to selling your business.

Price is only one of the deal terms involved in selling or buying a business. The seller is also interested in several other commitments from the buyer, such as timing and form of payment, what happens to business debt, and what happens to the employees. Meanwhile, the buyer is interested in getting financing, possibly excluding some assets or liabilities from the deal, and assurances that the business reality matches the seller's description.

When the buyer provides the non-binding Expression of Interest or the Letter of Intent, they include their positions on a number of considerations (deal terms). They might even organize their positions into an attached "term sheet." The buyer's offer is based on those positions. If the seller wishes to negotiate changes in those deal term positions (and he always does), the buyer reserves the right to change the offered price.

The following summary of terms assumes sale of the company intact. Some variations apply when the buyer is buying only the assets of the company.

Basic Buyer Deal Terms

In every deal, the seller should expect the buyer's deal terms to include those listed below, according to *The Acquisition Term Sheet—AccountingTools*:[35]

1. *Binding.* The term sheet will state whether the terms in the document are binding. Usually they are not, and it will go on to state that the terms are subject to the eventual negotiation of a purchase agreement.

2. *Parties.* This states the names of the acquirer and the target company.

3. *Price.* This is the total amount of consideration to be paid to the seller. There will probably be a clause saying that the stated price will change, depending upon information uncovered during due diligence.

4. *Form of payment.* This states whether the price will be paid in cash, debt, stock, or some mix of these elements.

5. *Earn-out.* If there is to be an earn-out, this clause states how the earn-out is to be calculated. See Article 12.3.

6. *Post-closing working capital adjustment.* This states any changes in the purchase price that will be triggered if the seller's working capital varies from a certain predetermined amount as of the closing date. See Article 13.4.

7. *Legal structure.* This states the form of the legal structure to be used, such as a triangular merger or an asset purchase. The legal structure can have profound tax implications for the seller, so this item may require considerable negotiation.
   – Some buyers will prefer to purchase only the assets rather than the stock of the business. Buying assets may enable them to avoid taking responsibility for most business liabilities, and allows them to start depreciation from a new basis. In contrast, buying the stock enables them to retain key contracts and avoid the need to perform a valuation on intellectual property assets. See Article 13.3.

8. *Escrow.* This states the proportion of the price that will be held in escrow, and for how long. See Article 13.3.

9. *Due diligence.* This states that the acquirer intends to conduct due diligence, and may state the approximate dates when this will occur. See Chapter 13.

10. *Responsibility for expenses.* This states that each party is responsible for its own legal, accounting, and other expenses related to the acquisition transaction.

11. *Closing.* This states the approximate date when the acquirer expects that the purchase transaction will close.

12. *Acceptance period.* This states the time period during which these terms are being offered. The recipient must sign the term sheet or offer letter within the acceptance period to indicate approval of the terms. Limiting the time of the offer allows the acquirer to later offer a different (usually reduced) set of terms if the first offer was not accepted and circumstances change.

Additional Buyer Deal Terms

1. *No shop provision.* The seller agrees not to disclose ("shop") the offered price to other prospective bidders in an effort to find a higher price. This clause can be legally binding.
   - The best situation for the seller is to have an auction involving several bidders. If this is the plan, sellers would not agree to a no-shop term until after selecting the most likely buyer among competing offers.

2. *Stock restriction.* If payment is to be in stock, the acquirer will likely require that the seller cannot sell the shares within a certain period of time, such as 6 or 12 months.

3. *Management incentive plan.* The buyer may offer a bonus plan, stock grants, stock option plan, or some similar arrangement for the management team of the seller. This clause is intended to quell any nervousness among the managers, and may gain their support for the deal.

4. *Non-compete.* Usually the buyer wants the seller to promise not to start-up or work for a competing concern within the same geography for a year or two, though such clauses can be difficult to enforce in the courts.

5. *Announcements.* Either party may feel that it would be damaging to announce the terms to the general public or news media, so this clause states that doing so must have the prior approval of the other party.

6. *Conditions precedent.* This states the requirements that must be met before the acquirer will agree to complete the purchase transaction. Examples of conditions precedent are having several years of audited financial statements, the completion of due diligence, the approval of regulatory agencies, the completion of any financing by the acquirer to obtain the funds to pay for the transaction, and the condition of the seller's company being substantially as represented. The acquirer includes these items in the term sheet or offer letter to provide a reasonable excuse to extricate himself. See Article 13.4.

7. *Representations and warranties.* This is a short statement that the acquirer will want representations and warranties from the seller in the purchase agreement. These clauses essentially create a warranty that the business is truly represented to the acquirer. See Article 12.4.

12.2 Key Deal Terms: Seller Financing

When you sell your small business, you want to echo Cuba Gooding Jr. in *Jerry Maguire:* "Show me the money!"[36] But small business owners typically do *not* receive the entire payment when the selling transaction closes. Wary buyers usually gain agreement to withhold some of the payment, to protect against the risk that the true picture is not as rosy as depicted by the seller. They want to motivate the seller to tell the truth and help them succeed. Negotiation of these payment-related deal terms is crucial to reaching agreement.

Three methods for holding back funds are seller financing, earn-out, and an escrow account for indemnification and post-purchase working capital adjustments. This article addresses seller financing. The next two articles address the other two payment-deferral methods.

Seller-Financing

"Seller financing is involved in up to 90 percent of small business sales, and more than half of mid-size sales," according to *Options for Financing Your Business Sale | BizFilings Toolkit.*[37] Buyers see seller financing as equivalent to a warranty by the seller, a bond that the business can perform as described. Sellers tend to be reluctant to offer financing, but the need to attract buyers by reducing the initial cash requirement usually leads sellers to accept the need to do so.

Other benefits of seller financing include a higher sale price, a speedier sale process compared to the time required for the buyer to get a bank loan, and the tax advantages of spreading the sale gains over several years.

Seller-financing is an agreement—written in a "promissory note" or financing agreement—that the buyer will pay to the seller some part of the purchase price plus interest on a regular basis over the next few years. Sellers can expect to finance 1/3 to 2/3 of the sale price. Interest rates tend to be less than bank loan rates, unless the buyer also has a bank loan (see below). The loan term is typically three to seven years, with monthly payments beginning 30 days after the sale, but the start of payments may be deferred if there is also a bank loan involved.

If there is no bank financing involved at the time of the sale, the seller note will often require a large "balloon payment" at the end of the term. This implies that the buyer will get bank financing after a few years, replacing the seller note with a bank loan, part of which is used to pay the balloon amount to the seller.

If the buyer is getting financing from a bank, the bank may require the seller to finance perhaps 25% of the purchase price. The bank hedges its risk when it requires the seller to risk his own money. The bank wants the seller to stand behind the valuation of the business by sharing in the risk of its future success.

Risks to the Seller

- If there is no bank loan and the seller is providing the only financing, the business itself will be the collateral, along with the buyer's personal guarantee. But if cash flow becomes so short that the payments are not being made, the value of the business will have diminished to become less than the value of the loan. So there is a risk of non-payment, and also a risk of insufficient collateral due to changes in its market value.

- If a bank loan is involved, the seller's financing usually is an unsecured loan, because the bank loan has a prior claim on all the business assets. So the seller has little recourse beyond the buyer's personal guarantee if payments are not made on schedule. In this case, the interest rate should be higher than bank rates, to reflect the risk of an unsecured loan.

- Because loan payments depend on the cash flow of the business, the seller who makes a loan still faces the risks of the business after selling it, yet no longer has control of its operations.

Reducing Risk with Seller-Financing

In addition to investigating the buyer's creditworthiness, obtaining a personal guarantee (including signature by the buyer's spouse), and charging a higher interest rate, other methods to reduce the seller's risk include:

- Requiring the buyer's other assets as collateral, to the extent they are not already pledged for other loans.

- Requiring the buyer to get life insurance or even disability insurance with the seller as beneficiary.

- Requiring the buyer to purchase an annuity contract or zero-coupon bonds for the seller. This means future installment payments of the purchase price would not be dependent on the success of the business. This method still reduces total buyer cash requirements because these instruments can be bought for less than their face value, i.e., their future payouts.

- Requiring the buyer to provide the seller with quarterly financial statements.

- Requiring that the loan is due in full immediately if the business does not meet certain performance levels on selected operating ratios ("loan covenants").

- Requiring seller approval before making material changes in the business (asset purchases, acquisitions, divestitures, expansions), and even the new owner's salary, until the loan is paid off.

- Requiring the buyer to form a corporation to purchase the business, and to pledge the stock of that corporation as collateral for the seller note. This enables the seller to take over the business and replace management in the event of non-payment, and do so much more quickly than the foreclosure process.

Buyers value seller financing as a warranty, and because it seems faster and easier than getting a bank loan. As a result, sellers often find that providing financing is the only way to find a buyer for their business. Given appropriate risk protections, seller financing can be a win-win deal term.

12.3 Key Deal Terms: Earn-out

The term "Earn-out" means that part of the purchase price of the business is paid to the seller only if the acquired company achieves specified financial or non-financial milestones during a specified period after the deal's closing date. Typical parameters are 30% of the stated purchase price and a two year period, according to Shareholder Representative Services LLC (https://www.shareholderrep.com/).[38] In their study, 15% of transactions included earn-out provisions, and it was uncommon for the earn-out period to extend beyond three years.

The metric for milestone achievement is normally percent change in gross sales or some earnings measurement. Most sellers prefer to base the earn-out on highest possible line of the income statement, ideally percent change in gross sales. Sellers prefer to avoid using earnings-based metrics because earnings depend on expense control, which is subject to management discretion (manipulation) for both amounts and timing. For example, the new owner could pay a large bonus to employees to reduce earnings, causing an earn-out milestone to be missed, resulting in no payment to the seller.

In contrast, buyers prefer to base the earn-out on earnings. In the SRS study, 89% of the milestones were financial, the most common financial measurement was EBITDA, and only 50% of earn-out metrics or milestones were actually achieved. EBITDA stands for Earnings Before Interest, Taxes, Depreciation, and Amoritization. It is basically Operating Margin plus Depreciation.

The earn-out agreement is often the compromise solution when the buyer and the seller have different views of the future value of the business. The buyer pays a minimum at the time of closing, and events determine the amount of the remainder paid later. For example, when the asking price is $2 million, the buyer may be willing to pay $1 million at closing plus 5% of gross sales over the next three years. Some earn-outs, such as this example, may offer some "upside potential" to the seller, i.e., the potential to be paid more than the asking price.

The most fundamental issue in negotiating an earn-out is identifying who will be managing the business after sale. Usually the buyer is the manager, but in some transactions a financial buyer will plan to depend on the seller to remain as the manager. The terms of the earn-out will be different if the person to be paid is also managing the results! This article assumes the buyer is managing the business.

Earn-out Benefits and Risks

Buyer	Seller
Benefits: • Resolves doubts about valuation • Less cash required at closing • Opportunity to integrate a motivated seller into business operations post-closing	Benefits: • Sale becomes more likely due to resolving different views on value and reducing cash required at closing • Lower taxes from deferring proceeds • Potential upside—higher total sale value
Risks: • Disputes, especially if the buyer wishes to transform the business • If seller is involved in the business post-closing, decisions may tilt toward short-term improvements jeopardizing long-term growth	Risks: • Retain risk without control • Limited access to business records • Potential manipulation of performance by the buyer • Disputes, especially if the buyer wishes to transform the business

Negotiating Earn-out Terms

The basic earn-out terms are:

- duration of the earn-out period

- the metrics to be used (there may be more than one)

- the way each metric is calculated

- level of performance that triggers payment

- amount of payment

Other critical matters must also be negotiated. These include:

- Number or frequency of payments, and the timing of the payment after a milestone is achieved.

- Any caps on total amount paid or amount paid per interval.

- Who calculates the metric? How can the seller verify actual performance vs. reported results?

- How will disputes be resolved?

- If the buyer wishes to sell the business within the earn-out period ("change of control"), will the seller be entitled to an accelerated earn-out payment? If so, how will it be calculated?

- Can the buyer deduct from future earn-out payments any indemnity claims exceeding the seller's agreed obligations (escrow)? See the next two articles for more about indemnification.

Advice to Sellers

Keep it simple! Negotiate for the shortest earn-out period, with only one or two metrics. The metrics should be carefully defined, because most earn-out disputes are based on the method of calculating the results achieved.[39]

Beware of earn-outs if the buyer plans to transform the business during the earn-out period, because such future changes create difficulty in agreeing on the proper measurement of milestone metrics, leading to disputes and payment delays. Examples of transformations are integrating the acquired business into the buyer's other businesses, entering new markets, and launching new products.

Stay involved to minimize your risk! You will want to have a consulting agreement so you can retain access to company records and remain aware of developments. If your key people are crucial to results, negotiate retention agreements with them before you sell.

Finally, pay attention to incentives. Negotiate so that the buyer will spend enough on capital investments and marketing, and will structure employee compensation to motivate the behaviors that achieve your milestone targets.

12.4 Key Deal Terms: Representations, Warranties, and Escrow

Ronald Reagan is famous for saying "Trust, but verify."[40] Representations, warranties, and escrow are the fundamental tools for describing the business and guaranteeing that the descriptions are true. They are used to make sure the seller tells the whole truth, because he loses a portion of the purchase price if his descriptions turn out to be untrue.

Buyers try to reduce the risk of unforeseen value destroyers when agreeing to purchase a business. Their goal is to get a clear and honest picture of the business from the seller. Prior articles showed how seller financing and earn-outs make payment of the purchase price depend on the post-sale success of the business. This motivates the seller to avoid painting an overly-optimistic picture to get a higher price, by reducing payments if the reality turns out to be less attractive.

Seller financing and earn-outs take years to play out, and deals may use one or the other but rarely both methods. Representations and warranties are a third method to achieve the same goal: an honest and complete understanding of the business liabilities before signing the Purchase Agreement. Reps and warranties claims are usually resolved in 12 to 18 months.[41] *Every* transaction will use representations and warranties.

Representations and Warranties

In the Purchase Agreement, Sellers make several statements to describe the business situation. These are called "representations" or "reps" for short. Textbooks list 32 possible reps![42] Some examples are absence of environmental liabilities, absence of tax liabilities, and clear rights to all your intellectual property. Some rep topics apply to all businesses, and others apply depending on the nature of the business being sold.

Buyers also offer reps and warranties about their own business and their personal net worth, but since the seller's reps are typically much more important to the deal, this article focuses only on seller reps.

Reps and warranties are contractual commitments from seller to buyer. The seller "warrants" (guarantees) they are true. This guarantee or warranty means a financial penalty to the seller if the statement is not true. Without that warranty, the buyer has no assurance that they can rely on those statements. So the two terms are almost always used together: "reps and warranties."

Indemnification

The indemnity section of the Purchase Agreement is where the parties agree to indemnify each other for inaccurate representations. Indemnify means one party pays the other to make up for the financial effect of such inaccuracies.

Escrow

Escrow is the method often used to implement the seller's indemnity, i.e., the warranty or guarantee.

Escrow uses a third party to receive money from the buyer, and to release it to the seller only when certain agreed conditions have been met. This tool gives the seller the comfort of knowing the buyer has committed the money. Meanwhile, it protects the buyer from the difficult task of recovering funds from the seller if it turns out the seller has not done everything he agreed to, or has made untrue representations about the business.

Escrow is used for several purposes, not just for indemnification. Escrow is used for earnest money, i.e., a deposit that might be made with the Letter of Intent. It is also used between signing the agreement and actually closing the transaction. The buyer's money can be paid to the escrow agent shortly after signing, and then released to the seller after closing conditions have been met to everyone's satisfaction.

Escrow can also be used to hold a portion of the purchase price until some number of months after the closing date, so the amount eventually paid to the seller can be reduced by the amount of indemnification due to the buyer.

Another use of the escrow account is to compensate either buyer or seller for a difference from the agreed net working capital (current assets minus current liabilities) of the business when the deal closes. Such differences are usually discovered shortly after the closing of the transaction. The same escrow account used for indemnification is also used to balance such Post-Purchase Adjustments (PPAs). See Article 13.4.

Importance of Reps, Warranties, and Indemnity Claims

Some statistics from SRS for sales of privately-held companies in 2012 show that sellers are wise to pay careful attention to reps, warranties, and indemnification:[43]

- The amount of the escrow account was more than 10% of the purchase price in over half these deals. The average range was 10 to 15%. For 3% of the deals, the escrow amount was 100% of the purchase price!

- The escrow holding period averaged 12 to 18 months.

- 98% of the deals contained "carve-outs," meaning that indemnity liability for certain matters lasts longer than the escrow holding period. Typical carve-outs involve sellers' ownership of shares, taxes, and fraud.

- 58% of the deals had escrow claims, usually reducing the funds eventually provided to the seller.

- Release of escrow funds was delayed due to claims in 30% of the deals, with the average delay being 7 months.

- Deals with delays had an average of 3.6 escrow claims.

- The most common sources of claims were tax and intellectual property issues.

- 72% of the deals with PPA mechanisms had a post-closing adjustment.

What Sellers Should Do

Reps and warranties, disclosures, and covenants are where your deal lawyer adds value. Wording choices and negotiations can have substantial effects on the amount eventually paid to the seller. The next article addresses some typical issues in these deal terms.

12.5 Key Deal Terms: Where Your Advisors Add Value

Buyers and sellers depend on three types of advisors:

* Business Broker or Investment Banker helps with valuation, the Offering Memorandum, finding and qualifying potential buyers, and advising on deal terms to satisfy both parties.

* Accountant prepares the business financial statements and advises on the formulation of deal terms which depend on financial metrics, such as earn-outs and post-purchase price adjustments.

* Business lawyer anticipates risks, drafts/negotiates the wording of deal terms to reduce risk, and ensures proper deal documentation.

* Both broker and attorney advise the seller concerning the sales process itself.

Representations and Warranties and "Disclosures"

The previous article defined reps and warranties as statements about the business that the seller warrants or guarantees are true. The seller agrees to pay the buyer (indemnifies the buyer) for the financial impact of any reps that turn out to be untrue.

Many of the most important reps are disclosure statements. They communicate that there are no liabilities in a particular subject area *except those disclosed* to the buyer, usually in an attachment to the deal documents.

The seller's promise of cash compensation guarantees the accuracy of the business description. The guarantee means money could change hands, so these deal terms are heavily-negotiated by the attorneys for both sides.

Not just any attorney will suffice. The seller's attorney should be experienced in buy/sell transactions for the seller's business size. This experience enables the attorney to minimize the seller's risk by quickly suggesting subtle wording changes, or by responding to the wording proposed by the buyer's experienced deal lawyer.

Disclosure Wording Issues

The seller's attorney tries to narrow the definitions in the disclosures. Examples:

- They are true, but only to the knowledge of the seller at the time they made the statement. The buyer wants them to be true according to what the seller *should have known* with reasonable investigation, and wants them to be true at closing as well as when first stated.

- Inaccuracies that are not significant should not matter. This threshold is called a "material adverse effect," and can be defined several ways. One issue is whether the inaccuracy materially affects the business now, or should its effect on the *prospects* of the business also be considered?

- The buyer wants the seller to have the duty to inform the buyer when the seller becomes aware that something in the disclosure statement is no longer true. The seller may accept this responsibility, but may want to limit it to things they are aware of, and only if those issues are material.

- Regarding the litigation disclosure, the buyer may want it to cover both pending and threatened litigation, while the seller wants to address only actual litigation already filed since they may not know of all pending or threatened suits.

Indemnity Wording Issues

The seller's attorney tries to limit the amount of the indemnity, the duration of the discovery period, and the complexity of the claims process. Examples:

- Seller wants to cap the total amount of the indemnity. Buyer does not.

- Seller wants a threshold of materiality before an indemnity claim is permitted. Buyer does not.

- Seller wants to pay only for damages beyond the threshold. Buyer wants payment from the first dollar.

- Buyer may want to introduce punitive damage claims as well as actual impact.

- Buyer will want some "carve-outs": seller liabilities that survive beyond the indemnity end date, or which carry different levels of potential liability. Seller does not. Sometimes the solution is indemnity "baskets" of different liability types or payment types.

Other Wording Issues

The seller's attorney will try to limit post-purchase price adjustments, such as by excluding unknown tax liabilities on pre-sale operations. The deal will also include "covenants": agreements by the buyer and seller that both will take (or not take) certain actions, usually between signing and closing. The most common examples are that neither will announce the deal without the other's permission, and that the seller will not "shop" the deal to other buyers to get a better price. The attorneys will seek agreement on wording that provides for certain exceptions to these covenants.

Chapter 13: From Due Diligence to Closing

13.1 Due Diligence: A Process Overview

Due diligence is the "verify" phase of the deal. In this phase the buyer gets the opportunity to verify the seller's "representations" about the results, potential, and risks of the business. The buyer will examine financial and other records to make sure there are no material (that is, having a major effect on value) issues or impairments that could limit the company's ability to operate at the level described by the seller.

If the buyer finds such issues, the seller should expect one or more of these responses: buyer offers a lower price; buyer seeks stronger guarantees and risk-sharing from the seller; or buyer walks away.

Due Diligence is where the seller's assurances are scrutinized. The seller provides the buyer with access to documents, and perhaps interviews and site visits as well. This information is highly confidential, so sellers allow buyers access only when a sale seems likely.

Prior to due diligence, the seller and buyer have reached this point in the overall sales process:

- The buyer has signed a Non-Disclosure (Confidentiality) Agreement.

- Deal terms and buyer concerns have been discussed in general, the seller has described the business and made representations about the company and its prospects, and the seller believes an agreement can be reached.

- The buyer has submitted a signed Letter of Intent (LOI) containing price and terms. The LOI usually qualifies the offer by making it subject to findings in due diligence.

- Often the buyer has submitted a list of the documents they wish to review in due diligence.

The Data Room

The seller enables due diligence by placing documents in binders for major topics, such as Financial, Legal, Operations, IT, and Personnel. The binders are shelved in a secure room, often located in the office of the seller's attorney. The attorney controls access to this "data room."

Buyers or their advisors will be allowed to review the documents at certain hours on certain days. If there are multiple potential buyers, each is scheduled for different days/times. A representative of the seller or their attorney will be present within or just outside the data room at these times.

Usually the seller allows the buyer to use computers to take notes about the documents, but does not permit buyers to make copies without special permission.

Seller's Preparation: "Think Like a Buyer"

The seller and their attorney must decide which documents to provide, so they can prepare the binders before due diligence begins. After preliminary negotiations, they will adapt the binder contents to address concerns expressed by the buyer. In choosing documents, their first thought will be to minimize disclosure of any information that might diminish the value of the business in the eyes of the buyer.

The danger in this attitude is that its pursuit of the highest price can prevent any deal at all! Buyers are getting expert advice, and they know what they're looking for. If they cannot find it, or it is incomplete, their confidence in the seller and the company may suffer enough that they walk away.

Buyers are looking for a trustworthy seller, a company with solid results, and opportunities to grow profits. They expect to pay a price reflecting those solid results and a portion of the growth opportunity, but hope to grow the business so its value significantly exceeds the price they paid. Thus company weaknesses that can be corrected by the buyer after the sale become opportunities for greater profits to the buyer.

A seller who tries to hide or downplay such weaknesses makes the company less attractive to buyers intent on growing profits!

Even worse, when a buyer finds those weaknesses anyway, their trust in the seller tumbles, and they begin to doubt everything else they've been told. If this happens, the deal may fall apart.

The best way to prepare for due diligence is to think like a buyer. Provide the basic documents supporting the assertions in the Offering Memorandum, or the list of requested documents provided by the buyer, but go further to anticipate the key issues buyers will want to learn more about. Such issues should not be difficult to anticipate:

- The seller already knows the company's main challenges.

- Consideration of fifteen areas of due diligence listed in the next article can reveal other risks that may concern buyers.

Assemble and be ready to provide documents to address these likely major concerns, if requested. Be prepared to discuss how the buyer can solve these issues, thereby adding value to his newly-acquired company. This is what "think like a buyer" means. Anticipate the buyer's concerns and offer solutions that will add value. Moreover, if the seller can implement some of those solutions before closing, a higher sales price may result.

The Buyer's Due Diligence Process

The buyer may review some documents in person, and may also delegate review of certain areas to an accountant or attorney. The buyer may create a "notes document" about each item reviewed, summarizing its content, any issues raised, and the potential risk or opportunity.

After the data room review is completed, the buyer may take some steps for follow-up due diligence:

- Submit a list of questions for clarification or discussion by the seller.

- Request site visits.

- Request permission to contact certain customers or suppliers, or even unions. Note that asking for permission is polite, but may not be needed if the buyer already knew of these customers or suppliers from sources other than the seller's confidential information.

When data-gathering is complete, the buyer will evaluate the findings for risks and opportunities, and will consider potential changes in deal terms to reduce risks. See Article 13.3 for more on this.

Seller's Due Diligence on the Buyer

The seller may request access to buyer information as seller's due diligence, to understand buyer qualifications in more depth than was possible when the buyer first expressed interest. The goal is the same as the buyer's goal: to reduce risk in the transaction. This is less common than buyer due diligence, so it is not the focus of this article.

13.2 Due Diligence Topics and Checklist

Sellers can use the following categories to organize the documents in their due diligence data room. Note that some of these documents may already have been shared and discussed prior to due diligence, but those documents need to be available in the data room anyway.

General Area	Financial	Legal	Operations	Information Systems (IT)	Personnel
Topic Area	– Financial – Insurance	– General Company – Corporate Agreements – Intellectual Property (IP) – Litigation – Environmental – Tax	– Customers – Marketing – Sales – Support Services – Products and Pricing – Processes and Production – Facilities	– Software – Hardware – Databases – Internal Controls	– Employees, Pay, Benefits, and other HR matters

Extensive checklists for documents can be found at *Due Diligence Checklist*.[44] Here is a summary description of the ideal documents for each of these topic areas, from the buyer's perspective.

Financial: Audited financial statements for three years; unaudited results for the current year; budgets vs. actuals for two years; other financial reports for three years; detailed capital expenditures (capex) for three years; receivables aging schedule; correspondence with auditors for three years; projected financial results for the next three years.

Insurance: Summaries of insurance policies including "key man" life insurance, property, general liability, vehicle, worker's compensation, employee health, and umbrella liability. Include the name of carrier, annual premium, coverage, claims over the last three years, self-insurance amounts reserved, co-payments/deductibles, and type of policy (occurrence vs. claims made).

General: List of subsidiaries; capitalization, number of shares, and owners; certificate of incorporation and bylaws; minutes of stockholder and board meetings including committees for three years; any other agreements among stockholders relating to management, ownership, loans, employment, or indemnity; all financing agreements; stock records; rights and warrants lists and the supporting agreements; address of all land and buildings; all material permits, licenses, government authorizations, and related correspondence; any other agreements with government entities except customer contracts.

Corporate Agreements: Borrowing agreements; credit line correspondence; acquisition and asset disposition agreements; joint venture, consulting, franchise, and other conditional agreements; distributor contracts; non-compete agreements; all other material contracts.

Intellectual Property: List of all trademarks, service marks, trade names, copyrights, and patents; evidence of registration, ownership, and/or first use of these; agreements concerning employee or outsider rights to products; procedures for maintaining trade secrets; end user license agreements; escrow agreements for computer source code; records of claims and disputes for IP; product literature made public in past two years; product maintenance logs and error reports for past 12 months.

Litigation: List of resolved litigation for past five years; summary of pending or threatened litigation; list of all attorneys acting for the company currently; summary and copies of all court and arbitration orders and settlements currently binding on the company.

Environmental: All permits and notices or demands from environmental authorities; written reports on environmental testing or other such matters; estimates of future remediation costs; records of compliance activities; location of all hazardous waste disposal sites; locations of all underground tanks and lines including those no longer used; any history of leakage or spillage from such facilities.

Tax: All tax returns from the last three years plus any open years; all information on past and pending audits and judgments concerning any open returns; tax waivers or collection agreements; all requests for rulings by taxing bodies; any material tax decisions or elections by management.

Customers and Marketing: List of top 20 customers with revenue billed and collected from them in past three years; total customers by product for past three years; number of monthly website visitors for past two years; description of sales channels per product and their percentage of revenue; target customers and marketing plan per product; description of sales organization and sales/purchase order process; key customer relationships; industry segment description including brand awareness and product introductions/success; competitive analysis including differentiation; customer base vs. that of competitors; strategic alliances.

Sales: Revenue from new customers for past three years; international sales revenue in total and for top ten countries for past three years; planned new product releases; description of significant new business and lost business; growth opportunities; major partnerships and their effect on revenue growth.

Pricing and Support Services: Explanation of the economics behind all fees and prices; level and source of margins per product and support service; significant customer contract terms; process for delivering upgrades to customers; discussion of product customization and effect on margins; description of the customer support function and its availability.

Processes and Production: Process maps for key processes; description of facilities, their role in production, and any significant expected facility upgrade or maintenance costs; list of critical raw materials and key suppliers, and their value and continuity; list of critical production skills and their continuity; utilization rate per asset and monthly utilization rates to show seasonality; percentage of invoices paid in full, percentage or value of warranty returns and key production metrics such as units per hour and percentage of hours devoted to rework; inventory turnover by type, and value and type of any inventory unused for 12 months.

Information Systems and Internal Controls: Describe software, hardware, and databases, and how they compare to those used by competitors; identify costs for such assets over the past three years, and any material future expenses expected; describe IT and Internet security, backups, remote records, and disaster recovery plans; describe accounting and financial controls and IT departmental functions.

Employees and HR: Union contracts and any related correspondence; management employment contracts or other agreements such as severance, consulting, and non-compete; organizational chart with names of function heads and number of subordinates; list of all employees earning over $100,000; employee benefit plans and related correspondence, reports, and filings; funding status and non-funded liability of each benefit plan; liability for termination payments to employees; details of other employee plans and arrangements; list of active and inactive employees for last three years with title, function, tenure, unique skills, and compensation; description of any order or decree applying to any senior executive which could affect the company's conduct of business.

13.3 Due Diligence and Deal Terms

What does the buyer *do* with all this due diligence information? After due diligence is complete, some buyers may decline to participate further, but most will seek agreement on deal terms that minimize the risks they verified or discovered in due diligence. They spent time and money to go through the document review process, so they are likely to seek solutions rather than simply walk away.

First, Buyers Assess Their Findings

After due diligence, buyers assess their findings. They list the risks and opportunities, and prioritize them according to financial impact. Together with their advisors, they may create several preliminary forecasts of business results. They'll use different scenarios for future outcomes of the most important risks and opportunities.

Second, Buyers Discuss Their Concerns with the Seller

Buyers will want to hear the seller's view of the risks and opportunities. The seller may clarify misunderstandings, point out connections among findings that change the risk assessment, or explain how current initiatives are expected to reduce the risks or take advantage of the opportunities. As a result, buyers change their assessments and preliminary forecasts.

Third, Buyers Seek Deal Terms to Minimize Risk and Optimize Opportunities

This step is the heart of deal negotiations. If buyers can gain protections or guarantees to back up the seller's assurances, the deal is likely to go forward. Buyers try to shift risk to the seller through deal terms. Methods may include seller guarantees (reps and warranties), exclusion of certain liabilities or assets, closing conditions, installment payment terms contingent on results, or reductions in the price offered.

Closing conditions require the seller to accomplish certain activities between signing the Agreement and actual transfer of ownership ("closing" the transaction). Examples of seller closing conditions include gaining government and lender approvals, release of liens, and gaining commitments from employees to remain with the business. The seller may also be asked to perform certain activities to make buyer synergy opportunities more likely to succeed. The next article is devoted to closing conditions.

Installment payment terms contingent on results include earn-outs, seller financing, and perhaps the seller's role in the business after sale.

Reps and Warranties

Buyers usually seek new or modified reps and warranties to make the seller responsible for risks identified in due diligence. These are usually limited to material (sizable) risks/costs discovered within a specified time after closing, such as 6 to 18 months. Four different approaches are:

- No risks: Seller states there are no risks of this type (e.g. product liability) and agrees to reimburse buyer for the cost of any that appear after closing. This is ideal for the buyer.

- No known risks other than those disclosed: Seller promises to reimburse buyer for any costs for risks the seller knew about *other than* those disclosed in an Appendix to the Purchase Agreement. The cost of disclosed risks is reflected in the agreed selling price.

- No risks seller should have known about other than those disclosed: Same as above, except seller's liability for disclosure is expanded to cover what a diligent manager *should* have known.

- Seller accepts liability to reimburse buyer for losses of a certain type up to a cap. For those costs not disclosed in the Appendix mentioned above, the seller's duty to reimburse the buyer is limited to a maximum amount, in addition to limitations on materiality and time discovered. Sellers prefer the certainty of a cap on potential future liabilities.

As noted earlier, the parties may agree that part of the purchase price is placed in escrow by the buyer to pay for any such liabilities discovered after closing.

Asset Sales

If the buyer believes liabilities of the business could be worth more than its assets, the offer could change from buying the business to buying only its assets. Buyers usually make this decision on deal structure earlier in the process, such as during preliminary deal term discussions after reviewing the Offering Memorandum. However, there have also been cases where due diligence findings caused buyers to change their deal structure strategy.

Buying only the assets leaves the original business (not the buyer) responsible for its own liabilities. Without its assets, the original business will cease operations and may declare bankruptcy to void the liabilities.

Buyers prefer an asset sale if there is a significant tax advantage due to restarting depreciation from a new basis—the price they paid for the assets. In contrast, when they purchase the business as a whole, they adopt its existing depreciation schedules, and some assets may already be fully depreciated. According to a recent ABA study, 87% of acquisitions were asset sales.[45]

The downside of asset sales is that they do not automatically include the business contracts and intellectual property, requiring separate valuation of these components if they are part of the assets purchased. Valuation of non-physical assets is not well-defined and thus can be an obstacle to reaching agreement.

Shifting the deal structure from sale of the business to sale of its assets changes the basis of valuation and price. In an asset sale, the price is no longer based on the value of future cash flows of the business as a whole. The price basis becomes the value of its assets if sold in the market today, whether sold together or piecemeal. Valuation and selling price are based on appraised value of assets rather than discounted cash flow analysis and multiples of comparable transactions.

In an asset sale, the parties must also agree on how much of the purchase price is allocated to each type of asset, including the premium over market value, called goodwill. Historically goodwill represents about 30% of the purchase price, though recently it has averaged only 19% according to an ABA survey.[46]

Exclusion of Certain Assets or Liabilities

Due diligence findings may show the buyer that certain assets of the business do not contribute to its future value. Examples include facilities with low utilization, inventory more than one year old, and machinery no longer used or duplicated by the buyer's machinery.

Buyers may also decide that certain liabilities can or must be retired by the seller prior to closing, to reduce the buyer's risk.

In such cases the buyer's remedy may be exclusion of such assets or liabilities from the purchase, perhaps with a corresponding change in purchase price. The Purchase Agreement may still apply to the business as a whole, but the unwanted assets or liabilities to be excluded would be listed in an Appendix.

Role of Advisors

Sellers may be shocked and dismayed by these dispassionate assessments of the components of the business. Often the seller has not assessed the business as a buyer would. The seller's advisors—attorney, investment banker/broker, and accountant—play an important role in these negotiations. They can help the seller see the reasons for the buyer's proposals, and suggest compromises based on experience in dozens of other transactions. Their counsel can enable the deal to be completed with a fair distribution of value and risk, rather than crumble into acrimony and rejection.

13.4 Closing Conditions

Most acquisitions do not close when the parties sign the Purchase Agreement. There is a time interval between signing and closing, often 90 days if regulatory approval does not require longer.

This interval enables the parties to complete some tasks to finalize the transaction, such as assignment of leases and buyer financing. However, it also adds complexity because the business is operating and changing in the meantime. Changes may include receivables and payables (working capital), customer contracts, employees, and other possibilities such as litigation.

To manage such risks, when they sign the Purchase Agreement the parties also negotiate and agree to a group of commitments, deliverables, and assurances concerning their actions between signing and closing. Together these are called "closing conditions." If these commitments are not satisfied by the responsible party by the closing date, the other party has the right to refuse to complete the transaction.

Promised Pre-Closing Behaviors (Covenants)

- Seller will not create a competing company, hire employees from the business into another business, or solicit customers to move to another supplier ("non-compete" and "non-solicit"). This covenant usually lives on for a stated period after closing.

- Seller will not seek or negotiate with other buyers ("no shop").

- Seller will get the buyer's approval before taking actions that could materially change the value of the business, such as limiting normal capital investment, acquiring or divesting major assets, or signing major contracts with customers, employees, or suppliers. Buyer's response will be timely and reasonable.

* Seller may be required to take certain actions that would enable the buyer to take advantage of opportunities more quickly after the sale.

* Neither party will announce the transaction or its details without the other party's agreement unless required to do so by law or regulation.

Assurances about Condition of the Business at Closing (Reps and Warranties)

* All reps and warranties agreed to at signing are true at closing, subject to materiality and knowledge qualifiers negotiated earlier, except as disclosed in updates to disclosure schedules. *This "bring-down" condition is the most important closing condition, and will be covered in more detail later in this article.*

* All covenants governing behavior between signing and closing have been complied with.

* No changes with material adverse effects on the business have occurred since signing.

* No litigation has started which would restrain or prohibit the transaction.

* Buyer guarantees to take certain post-closing actions, such as continuing employee benefit plans for a specified period, providing D&O insurance for the seller for a specified period, changing titles on assets, and cooperating on the

post-closing working capital adjustment to be completed by a certain date. *This latter item is the other highly-important closing condition, addressed later in this article.*

Deliverables (Documents)

* Stockholder and Board of Directors consents to the transaction as agreed.

* Corporate Secretary's certificate as to accuracy of company formation and capitalization documents.

* Regulatory approvals, licenses, permits, etc.

* Ancillary agreements such as seller financing and employee retention agreements.

* Third party consents, such as leases and assignment of contracts to the buyer.

* Release of liens and settlement of litigation.

* Standard deal documents, such as bill of sale for assets and escrow agreement.

Termination Rights

The transaction can be terminated

* If both parties agree to do so.

* If a legal impediment makes the transaction illegal.

* By one party if the other has not completed its closing conditions by a "drop-dead date."

* By one party if the other has materially breached a rep/warranty or failed to perform according to a covenant, after an agreed "cure" period (such as 30 days) to make it right.

"Bring-Down" of Reps and Warranties

The parties and their attorneys will burn plenty of negotiation calories defining which changes in the business since signing allow the buyer to walk away without closing. Materiality issues will include the threshold over which a change in one rep will be considered material, the threshold for the total of all changes before the total can be considered material, and whether the seller can exclude changes from this tabulation by updating disclosure schedules. Sellers want flexibility without enabling the buyer to change the agreed price or walk away, and buyers want the right to do both for the lowest possible materiality threshold.

Post-Closing Working Capital Adjustment

The working capital adjustment is the most common source of post-closing disputes. At signing, the Purchase Agreement uses an estimated figure for working capital, and promises that the actual figure for the closing date will be calculated 60 to 120 days after closing. The difference is paid out of escrow to the seller if actual exceeds estimate, or to the buyer if actual is less than the estimate. This process is called a "true-up."

Working capital is usually defined as current assets (cash, inventory, accounts receivable, and prepaid items) minus current liabilities (accounts payable and accrued expenses). The parties can minimize disputes if they define all these terms clearly in the agreement, if the definitions follow accepted accounting principles, and if the seller has the right to examine pertinent company records after the closing as part of the "true-up" process.

Conclusion

THIS BOOK IS ABOUT HOW TO GROW PROFITS through employees, revenue growth, and better operations.

If you make these techniques work, you'll have something to sell: a business, not a hobby and not just a product. You will have an increasingly profitable business with good growth prospects based on special ways of meeting customer needs. At some point you will want to sell the business and move on, so the book concludes by explaining the process for selling your business.

The path to growth is marked by decision-points. Do you "go big" or take the "one step at a time" approach? Where do you get advice? Can you trust it? Part Four offered some techniques for making these big decisions, and for negotiating successfully.

Making decisions is one of the biggest challenges facing small business owners, and they usually face this challenge alone. People are always around, but there is no one else to make the decision for you, and often no confidante who understands the business well enough to deliver the solution. Advisors are expensive, and you fear their advice is too general to be worth the money.

This book provides the trusted outside perspective that small business decision-makers have been missing. It collects and explains practical techniques to help them make the right decisions, based on 40 years of management and consulting experience. This book is designed to be your toolbox and guide to "master difficulties and win opportunities."[47]

See the following few pages for a full list of the techniques presented in this book. I hope you find at least some of them useful in your business! If you do, please keep up to date with *new* blog articles published weekly on Business Techniques in Troubled Times. Sign up for weekly emails of fresh articles at *www.tom-gray.com/blog-2/*.

Herb Kelleher, former CEO of Southwest Airlines, has a great quote to take us from considering to doing: "We have a strategic plan. It's called doing things."[48]

So do some things to make your business better!

Share what works by posting a comment on the blog, and contact Tom Gray at *tgray@tom-gray.com* for personal advice on techniques to solve your business problems.

Index of Topics and Techniques

Topic	Technique	Content	Articles
Motivation	3 Drivers	Opportunity for achievement, trust, appreciation.	1.1
	Demotivation	How you show disrespect.	1.2
Compensation	Salary Principles	Not a motivator; find the market rate.	2.1
	Salary Increases	Market rate; fairness; not a reward for longevity.	2.1
	Incentive Plans	Plan design: standard and points approaches.	2.2
	Non-Cash Rewards	Best motivator; list of 30.	2.3
Improving Employee Performance	Start with Vision	Vision, Buy-in, roles.	3.1
	Breakthrough Conversation	Get to know employees; how they do their jobs; what obstacles; remove and measure change.	3.2
	Delegate	Why it works; write methods first; train; how to introduce; incentives.	3.3
	Train	First write the method; train and demonstrate; job aid; graphic for guidance.	3.4
	Monitor and Coach	Monitoring form and how to use it.	3.5
	Collective Accountability	Why most incentive pay should be based on team, not individual, performance.	3.6
	Goal-setting	Why stretch goals; how to handle shortfalls.	3.7

	Appraisals	Work to upgrade your best people, not your worst.	3.8
	Management System	Aligning measurements and rewards with vision, strategy, and individual goals.	3.9
	Hiring People	Job description, Interview, Orientation, and 90-Day plan.	3.10
	Manage through Leaders	Identifying and developing them; managing through them.	3.11
	Learning from Staff Losses	Three most common reasons why people leave; it could be you! Survey attitudes regularly.	3.12
Growth Goals and Levers	Profit Assessment	Compare returns to other uses of your funds; calculate target return.	4.1
	Business Growth Machine	Understand levers for growth, and timing to expect.	4.2, 4.3
Low Risk Growth Levers	Quick Wins	For results in 30 days, use price increase and cost controls.	5.1
	Grow revenue from current customers	Depends on customer database. Consider loyalty club, merchandising, product bundles, volume packaging, promotions, and events.	5.2
	Change approach to attract new customers	Differentiation, positioning, new segment, credibility, message, customer experience.	5.3
	Promotional Readiness	Make a list. Involve everyone. How the team works.	5.4
	Competitor's new product	Raise prices when they do.	5.5
Moderate Risk Growth Levers	New Target Segment	Choosing an attractive segment.	6.1

Negotiating Skills	Research first	Know the topic, the other party, and two other suppliers. Choose your BATNA and threshold, and estimate the other's. Figure out their interest, often different from their position.	8.1
	Plan your solutions	Identify the decision-maker. Seek win/win. Respond off-target. Decide what to yield.	8.2
	Plan your behavior	Trading concessions. Who is first to mention price? Tone, listening, questions, non-verbal cues.	8.2
Decision-Making Skills	Making good decisions	Delegate; get advice.	9.1
	Use a Framework	How to use a 7 step approach.	9.2
	Assessing Alternatives	How to assess assumptions, advisor opinions, and your own. Change assumptions, find alternatives, and test.	9.3
	Dealing with Ethics and Resistance	Feel the impact on others, and use imagination to tweak for their benefit. Handle resistance privately, as a joint effort to improve the solution.	9.4
	Checklist for good decision-making	11 techniques.	9.5
Selling Your Business: Overview and Preparation	Overview	Describes five stages of the selling process, including role of business broker.	10.1
	Valuation	Two valuation methods: comparables and discounted cash flow. Identifies discounts for industry and company.	10.2

Due Diligence Overview	Explains the due diligence process. Recommends the seller's attitude and preparation.	13.1
Due Diligence Checklist	Lists dozens of types of documents which may be sought by buyers, in five categories.	13.2
Due Diligence and Deal Terms	Explains what the buyer does with due diligence findings. Techniques involve reps and warranties, asset sales, and exclusion of selected assets or liabilities.	13.3
Closing Conditions	Lists various closing conditions and deliverables. Techniques include "bring-down" of reps and warranties, and working capital adjustment.	13.4

References

1   *http://jamesaquilone.com/101-greatest-george-carlin-quotes/.*

2   *http://www.imdb.com/title/tt0080487/quotes.*

3   Thomas H. Gray, *Business Techniques in Troubled Times*, Thomas H. Gray, Inc., Lisle, Illinois, 2013.

4   *http://catherinescareercorner.com/2012/12/02/30-non-cash-rewards-to-give-at-work/.*

5   *http://www.tom-gray.com/blog-2/.*

6   *http://www.worksystems.com/freeResources/workforcePerformance/accountability.html.*

7   Ibid.

8   *http://www.imdb.com/character/ch0011720/quotes.*

9   *http://www.worksystems.com/newsletter/february_09.pdf.*

10 *http://unlockit.com/RefHM.html.*

11 Wayne Calloway, CEO of PepsiCo, quoted in *Fortune*, November 27, 1995.

12 John Bookout, CEO of Shell Oil, quoted in *Fortune*, January 19, 1987.

13 *http://www.worksystems.com/freeResources/workforcePerformance/
    get_employees_to_stay.html.*

14 *http://pages.stern.nyu.edu/~%20adamodar/New_Home_Page/
    datafile/histretSP.html.*

15 *http://lyndit.com/2010/02/25-inspiring-quotes-on-creativity/.*

16 Thomadsen, Raphael, "You Can Benefit from a Rival's New
    Product," *Harvard Business Review*, April 2013.

17 *http://www.newmarketsadvisors.com/findenternewmarkets/.*

18 Ibid.

19 Jay Heizer and Barry Render, *Operations Management*, Prentice
    Hall, 2011, page 157–8.

20 *http://www.uww.edu/wisc/.*

21 *http://chohmann.free.fr/5S/wastes.htm.*

22 *http://chohmann.free.fr/5S/index_us.html.*

23 *http://commfaculty.fullerton.edu/lester/writings/letters.html.*

24 *http://www.six-sigma-material.com/Process-Maps.html.*

25 *http://search.comcast.net/?cat=web&con=beta&form_submit
    =1&q=slideshare+process+mapping&top_SearchSubmit=.*

26 *http://www.balancedscorecard.org/Portals/0/PDF/bpihndbk.pdf.*

27 *http://www.gqc.org.au/Forum_2013_04_Presentation_1.pdf.*

28 James P. Womack and Daniel T. Jones, *Lean Thinking: Banish
    Waste and Create Wealth in Your Corporation,"* Free Press, New
    York, 1996, page 16.

29 Womack and Jones, *op. cit.* Eliyahu Goldratt and Jeff Cox,
    The Goal, third revised edition, North River Press, Great
    Barrington, MA., 2004. Mike George, Dave Rowlands, and

Bill Kastle, *What is Lean Six Sigma,* McGraw-Hill, New York, 2004. Craig Gygi, Neil DeCarlo, and Bruce Williams, *Six Sigma for Dummies*, Wiley Publishing Inc., Hoboken, NJ, 2005.

30 Roger Fisher and William Ury, *Getting to Yes: Negotiating Agreement Without Giving In*, Penguin Group, New York, 1981.

31 *http://www.brainyquote.com/quotes/quotes/m/miketyson382439 .html.*

32 *http://www.mckinsey.com/insights/strategy/making_great_decisions.*

33 *http://www.slayerment.com/blog/top-inspirational-motivational-quotes-all-time.*

34 *http://www.divestopedia.com/2/1041/maximize-value/company-premium/master-ten-value-drivers-to-sell-your-business-at-the-highest-price.*

35 *http://www.accountingtools.com/acquisition-term-sheet.*

36 *http://www.dailymotion.com/video/x17h1ey_cuba-gooding-jr-scene-show-me-the-money-jerry-maguire-1996_shortfilms.*

37 *http://www.bizfilings.com/toolkit/sbg/run-a-business/exiting/options-for-financing-business-sale.aspx.*

38 *https://www.shareholderrep.com/.*

39 Ibid.

40 *http://voices.yahoo.com/wise-ronald-reagan-quotes-could-improve-your-4551261.html.*

41 *https://www.shareholderrep.com/.*

42 Martin D. Ginsburg and Jack S. Levin, *Mergers, Acquisitions, and Buyouts*, four volumes, Aspen Publishers, New York, 2006.

43 *https://www.shareholderrep.com/.*

44 *http://www.duediligencedataroom.com/Checklist.html.*

45 *http://www.slideshare.net/MMMTechLaw/2011-purchase-agreement-study.*

46 Ibid.

47 *http://www.brainyquote.com/quotes/quotes/w/winstonchu156886 .html.*

48 *http://impactstartups.com/we-have-a-strategic-plan-its-called-doing-things-herb-kelleher/.*

About the Author

Tom Gray helps small business owners save and grow their companies, from planning and financing to marketing, pricing, and process improvement. He is a management consultant, MBA Professor, and author with several credentials: Certified Turnaround Professional (CTP), Certified Business  Development Advisor, and Certified SCORE Mentor.

His small business positions include President of his own consulting firm, interim CEO at two small NASDAQ companies, member of their Boards of Directors, and former Co-Chair of the Pro Bono Committee of the Turnaround Management Association, Midwest Region. His 30 year career at Ameritech included operations, marketing, strategy, and international M&A.

In addition to consulting, Tom writes a weekly blog about small business profit improvement techniques. His books include *Business Techniques in Troubled Times: A Toolbox for Small Business Success* (2013), and *Leadership in Kidney Care: the NANI Story* (2011). His degrees include an MA in History and an MBA. Tom and his wife Nancy live in Lisle, Illinois. For more information, see *www.tom-gray.com*.

28038013R00179

Made in the USA
Charleston, SC
30 March 2014